How to use your Snap Revision Text Guide

This 'A Christmas Carol' Snap Revision Text Guid̶ will help you get a top mark in your AQA English Literature exam. It is divided into ̶ ̶ ̶ ̶ ̶ so that you can easily find help for the bits you find tricky. This book ̶ ̶ ̶ ̶ o know for the exam:

Plot: what happens in the novel?

Setting and Context: what periods, places, events and attitudes are relevant to understanding the novel?

Characters: who are the main characters, how are they presented, and how do they change?

Themes: what ideas does the author explore in the novel, and how are they shown?

The Exam: what kinds of question will come up in your exam, and how can you get top marks?

To help you get ready for your exam, each two-page topic includes:

Key Quotations to Learn
Short quotations to memorise that will allow you to analyse in the exam and boost your grade.

Summary
A recap of the most important points covered in the topic.

Sample Analysis
An example of the kind of analysis that the examiner will be looking for.

Quick Test
A quick-fire test to check you can remember the main points from the topic.

Exam Practice
A short writing task so you can practise applying what you've covered in the topic.

Glossary
A handy list of words you will find useful when revising 'A Christmas Carol' with easy-to-understand definitions.

AUTHOR:
PAUL BURNS

ebook

To access the ebook version of this Snap Revision Text Guide, visit
collins.co.uk/ebooks
and follow the step-by-step instructions.

Published by Collins
An imprint of HarperCollins*Publishers*
1 London Bridge Street
London SE1 9GF

© HarperCollins*Publishers* Limited 2017

ISBN 9780008247119

First published 2017

10 9

British Library Cataloguing in Publication Data.

A CIP record of this book is available from the
British Library.

Commissioning Editor: Gillian Bowman
Managing Editor: Craig Balfour
Author: Paul Burns
Copyeditor: David Christie
Proofreaders: Jill Laidlaw and Louise Robb
Project management and typesetting:
  Mark Steward
Cover designers: Kneath Associates and
  Sarah Duxbury
Production: Natalia Rebow
Printed in the UK by Martins the Printer Ltd.

ACKNOWLEDGEMENTS

The author and publisher are grateful to the
copyright holders for permission to use quoted
materials and images.

Every effort has been made to trace copyright
holders and obtain their permission for the use
of copyright material. The author and publisher
will gladly receive information enabling them
to rectify any error or omission in subsequent
editions. All facts are correct at time of going
to press.

MIX
Paper from
responsible source
FSC
www.fsc.org   FSC™ C007454

This book is produced from independently
certified FSC™ paper to ensure responsible
forest management.

For more information visit:
www.harpercollins.co.uk/green

Contents

Stave (Chapter) 1

You must be able to: understand what happens at the beginning of the novel.

What is the setting?

The novel is set mainly in London at the time the novel was written (1843). The chapter opens in Scrooge's 'counting house' or office in the city and ends in his house.

What is the situation?

Ebenezer Scrooge is a businessman. His partner in the business, Jacob Marley, has been dead for seven years. Scrooge is known for his love of money and his meanness. When the novel opens, it is Christmas Eve and Scrooge and his clerk (Bob Cratchit) are still working at the counting house.

What happens?

The focus is mainly on Scrooge, as it is throughout the novel. The writer describes his appearance and nature, and other people's reactions to him. His attitude to Bob Cratchit is shown by his refusal to let him have a proper fire on a very cold day.

Scrooge is visited by his nephew Fred, who wishes him 'Merry Christmas', to which he replies 'Bah … Humbug'. They give their different views on Christmas. Despite Scrooge's **attitude**, Fred invites him to Christmas dinner with him and his new wife.

Scrooge is then visited by two 'portly gentlemen', who are collecting money to give to the poor. Scrooge says their situation is none of his business and refuses to give.

As the weather gets worse, Scrooge chases away a carol singer. He lets the clerk, Bob Cratchit, go home and reluctantly agrees he can have Christmas Day off. He then goes for a meal on his own before going home.

What changes the situation?

When he gets home, Scrooge begins to see and hear strange things. He tells himself it must be something he ate.

He hears a loud clanking noise approaching. He sees the ghost of his old partner, Jacob Marley, dragging a long chain behind him.

Marley tells him that, because of his behaviour in life, he has been condemned to walk the earth as a ghost.

He warns Scrooge that he could suffer the same fate and tells him that he will be visited by three spirits, who will help him avoid this fate.

Key Quotations to Learn

'Every idiot who goes about with "Merry Christmas" on his lips should be boiled with his own pudding and buried with a stake of holly through his heart.' (Scrooge)

'Are there no prisons?' asked Scrooge.

'Bah ... Humbug!' (Scrooge)

Summary

- Scrooge is a rich but very mean businessman who does not like Christmas.
- He argues with his nephew about the meaning of Christmas and rejects his friendship.
- He refuses to give any money to help the poor.
- He is visited by the ghost of his partner Jacob Marley, who warns him of what will happen after his death if he does not change.

Questions

QUICK TEST
1. Why does Scrooge's nephew visit him?
2. Why do the two gentlemen visit Scrooge?
3. Who was Marley and what is the result of his behaviour when he was alive?
4. What is the purpose of the spirits visiting Scrooge?

EXAM PRACTICE
Using at least one of the 'Key Quotations to Learn', write a paragraph explaining how Dickens conveys Scrooge's attitude to Christmas.

You must be able to: understand what happens in Stave 2.

What is the setting?

The chapter opens in Scrooge's bedroom. The Ghost of Christmas Past takes Scrooge back in time to earlier Christmases in different places.

What is the situation?

Scrooge wakes up in bed. He hears the clock striking twelve (midnight), although he went to bed at 2 am.

As the clock strikes one, Scrooge has a visit from a strange figure with a bright light coming from its head.

This figure, or spirit, is the Ghost of Christmas Past. The spirit says that it is the ghost of Scrooge's past and has come to help him.

What happens next?

The Ghost takes Scrooge to a place in the country that he recognises from his childhood.

They go into a school and see Scrooge as a boy. He is the only boy left there in the Christmas holidays. Scrooge weeps.

They see a group of colourful characters from books Scrooge read as a child. Scrooge is excited but becomes upset again, thinking about his boyhood. He remembers the young carol singer he turned away.

The Ghost shows him a later Christmas in the same place. They see Scrooge's sister, Fan. She tells young Scrooge that things are better at home and their father wants him to come home forever.

Scrooge tells the Ghost that Fan died as a young woman, leaving one child, his nephew.

Next, the Ghost shows Scrooge a Christmas when he was a young man. His old employer, Mr Fezziwig, and his wife have a big party for all their friends and employees. Old Scrooge relives every minute.

When the party is over, the Ghost and Scrooge talk about how easy it was for Fezziwig to make people happy and what a good employer he was. Scrooge thinks about his own clerk, Bob Cratchit.

The Ghost shows him a young woman (his **fiancée**, Belle) talking to Scrooge a few years later. She tells him that he now loves money more than he loves her and, because she is now poor, she thinks he does not want to marry her. She breaks off the engagement.

Scrooge tells the spirit that he does not want to see anything else but the spirit shows him one last scene. It is Belle, a bit older and surrounded by her children. She is very happy.

Her husband comes home and tells her that he has seen Scrooge and that he is 'quite alone in the world'.

How does the stave end?

Scrooge is upset and demands that the Ghost takes him home. He tries to put out the light that comes from the Ghost but fails.

Key Quotations to Learn

'A solitary child, neglected by his friends, is left there still.' Scrooge said he knew it. And he sobbed.

'I should like to be able to say a word or two to my clerk just now.' (Scrooge)

'Another **idol** has displaced me …' (Belle)

Summary

- The Ghost of Christmas Past shows Scrooge some of his past Christmases.
- As a child, Scrooge was lonely but found escape in books.
- He had a sister, Fan, who later died, leaving a child.
- When Scrooge was a young clerk he was happy working for generous Mr Fezziwig.
- Scrooge was engaged to be married but his fiancée broke the engagement because he was only interested in money.
- Scrooge is upset by what he is shown and begins to show emotion.

Questions

QUICK TEST
1. What is unusual about the spirit's head?
2. Who is the boy that Scrooge sees in the school?
3. What is the relationship between Fan and Scrooge's nephew?
4. Who does Scrooge think about when he has seen Mr Fezziwig's Christmas party?
5. Why does Belle release Scrooge from their engagement?

EXAM PRACTICE
Using at least one of the 'Key Quotations to Learn', write a paragraph showing how Scrooge has changed since his childhood.

You must be able to: understand what happens in Stave 3.

What is the setting?

The chapter starts in Scrooge's bedroom. The Ghost of Christmas Present takes him to various places: the Cratchits' house; his nephew's house; and other places where Christmas is being celebrated.

What is the situation?

Scrooge wakes up and it is one o'clock in the morning again. He sees a light coming from the next room and goes in. There, he finds the Ghost of Christmas Present, surrounded by food and Christmas decorations. Scrooge tells him he has learned a lesson and is willing to learn more.

What happens?

The Ghost shows Scrooge the streets of London, where everyone is preparing for Christmas. He helps to create a good mood by sprinkling people with **incense** from the torch he carries.

They go to the home of Scrooge's clerk, Bob Cratchit. Bob's wife and children are getting ready for Christmas dinner. Bob comes in from church carrying his son, Tiny Tim, who is ill.

The Cratchits have their Christmas dinner and Scrooge sees how much they appreciate it despite their poverty.

Scrooge asks the Ghost whether Tiny Tim will live. He replies that he will not live unless things change.

As it gets dark, the Ghost takes Scrooge through the streets and across the country, showing him miners, sailors and lighthouse keepers celebrating Christmas.

They go to the home of Scrooge's nephew, Fred. He, his wife and their friends are having a party. They sing and play games, having some fun at Scrooge's expense. Scrooge is happy watching them and wants to stay longer.

How does the stave end?

Scrooge notices the Ghost is getting older. The Christmas holidays are over. Two miserable and monstrous looking children appear from under the Ghost's cloak. He tells Scrooge that they are Ignorance and Want (poverty), the children of Man. When Scrooge asks him whether anything can be done for them, he reminds him of what he said to the portly gentlemen about **workhouses**.

The Ghost of Christmas Past disappears, the clock strikes twelve and another spirit appears.

Key Quotations to Learn

'God bless us every one!' said Tiny Tim.

'Mr Scrooge!' said Bob. 'I'll give you Mr Scrooge, the founder of the feast!'

'Are there no prisons?' said the Spirit, turning on him for the last time with his own words. 'Are there no workhouses?'

Summary

- The Ghost of Christmas Present shows Scrooge the Cratchits' Christmas.
- He tells Scrooge that Tiny Tim will die if nothing changes.
- The Ghost shows Scrooge his nephew, Fred, enjoying Christmas with family and friends. Scrooge is happy and lighthearted.
- Before disappearing, the Ghost shows Scrooge two monstrous children, who **symbolise** Ignorance and Want.

Questions

QUICK TEST
1. How does Scrooge feel about going with the Ghost of Christmas Present?
2. Who is Tiny Tim?
3. What does Scrooge ask the Ghost about Tim?
4. How does Scrooge react to Fred's party?
5. What are the children that emerge from the Ghost's cloak?

EXAM PRACTICE
Using at least one of the 'Key Quotations to Learn', write a paragraph explaining how Dickens conveys the **atmosphere** of Christmas.

Stave (Chapter) 4

You must be able to: understand what happens in Stave 4.

What is the setting?

The action takes place in the city of London. Scrooge is taken to the **Exchange**, where he works, to a shop in a run-down part of the city, to his house and office, to the Cratchits' house and, finally, to a graveyard.

What is the situation?

Scrooge has been left in the street by the Ghost of Christmas Present. He sees a **phantom**, covered in a black cloak and hood, with only one outstretched arm visible. The phantom is silent but Scrooge knows it is the Ghost of Christmas Yet to Come.

What happens?

The Ghost shows Scrooge visions of the future. First, it shows him some businessmen, whom he recognises, discussing someone's funeral. They are not upset about the man's death.

Scrooge does not understand why the Ghost is showing him this but decides to remember it and learn from it.

They then go to a shop in a poor part of town. Here, an **undertaker**, a **charwoman** and a **laundress** have brought things to sell to the shopkeeper. Scrooge realises all the items have been stolen from a dead man. He is horrified and disgusted by their actions.

He is shown the dead man, lying alone on his bed. He does not have the courage to look at the man's face but vows that he will learn from his fate.

He asks the Ghost to show him someone who feels emotion over the man's death. He sees a young couple. They are in debt to the dead man and are happy that he is dead because their future will be better.

Scrooge now wants to see some tenderness associated with death and is taken to the Cratchits' house. Tiny Tim has died and the family is mourning him. Bob says that he has seen Scrooge's nephew, who he knows will be kind to them. They remember Tiny Tim's goodness.

How does the stave end?

Scrooge asks who the dead man is. He is taken past his old office to a graveyard. The Ghost shows him a gravestone with his own name on.

Scrooge asks if he can avoid this fate and says he has learned from the three spirits and will change his life.

The Ghost disappears.

Key Quotations to Learn

... he viewed them with a detestation and disgust ... (Scrooge)

'It would have done you good to see how green a place it is.' (Bob Cratchit)

The finger pointed from the grave to him, and back again. (Scrooge)

Summary

- Scrooge is shown some businessmen talking about someone's death.
- He sees people selling the dead man's belongings.
- The only people who feel any emotion about the man's death are glad that he is dead.
- The Ghost shows him the Cratchits mourning for Tiny Tim.
- The Ghost reveals that the dead man is Scrooge. Scrooge says he has learned from the spirits and begs for a chance to change.

Questions

QUICK TEST
1. Who is the cloaked and hooded figure that appears to Scrooge?
2. What are the occupations of the three people in the shop?
3. How does Scrooge react to them?
4. What has happened to Tiny Tim?
5. Who is the dead man that Scrooge is shown?

EXAM PRACTICE
Using at least one of the 'Key Quotations to Learn', write a paragraph about how Dickens conveys different reactions to the deaths of Scrooge and Tiny Tim.

Stave (Chapter) 5

You must be able to: understand what happens at the end of the novel.

What is the setting?
Scrooge is back in the present. It is Christmas morning.

What is the situation?
The Ghost of Christmas Yet to Come has changed into one of Scrooge's bedposts. He wakes up happy to see that everything is as it was. He is determined to change and grateful to the spirits for giving him the chance to change.

What happens?
Scrooge is happy and excited, shouting, laughing and dancing as he gets dressed and looks around his house.

He looks out of his window and asks a boy in the street what day it is. When he says it is Christmas Day, Scrooge realises that everything has happened in one night. He sends the boy to buy a big prize turkey and then sends him in a cab to take it to Bob Cratchit.

Scrooge goes out. In the street, he meets one of the 'portly gentlemen' whose approach he rejected in Stave One. He promises him a large donation. He goes to church and then enjoys a walk through the city.

After nervously passing the house a few times, he knocks on his nephew's door. Fred and his wife welcome him and he enjoys the party.

The next day, he waits for Bob in his office and, when he enters, pretends to be annoyed. Bob apologises for being late but Scrooge tells him that he will give him a rise in his salary and help his family. Bob thinks he has gone mad.

How does the novel end?
We are told he is 'better than his word', Tiny Tim does not die and Scrooge is a changed man.

Key Quotations to Learn

Best and happiest of all, the Time before him was his own, to make amends in!

Scrooge was better than his word. He did it all and infinitely more; and to Tiny Tim, who did NOT die, he was a second father.

... and it was always said of him that he knew how to keep Christmas well ...

Summary

- Scrooge wakes up on Christmas morning, happy and determined to change.
- He sends a huge turkey to the Cratchits.
- He spends a happy Christmas with his nephew and family.
- He looks after the Cratchits and is a changed man for the rest of his life.

Questions

QUICK TEST
1. What day is it when Scrooge wakes up?
2. What does he send the boy to buy?
3. Where does he spend Christmas Day?
4. What does he promise Bob Cratchit?

EXAM PRACTICE
Using at least one of the 'Key Quotations to Learn', write a paragraph explaining what you think Dickens means by keeping Christmas well.

Narrative Structure

You must be able to: explain the significance of the different ways Dickens has structured the novel.

How is the novel structured?

The novel is divided into five chapters, which Dickens calls 'staves'. A stave is a musical term, which means the same as a **stanza** or verse.

Dickens used 'stave' to remind readers that he was writing a **prose** version of a Christmas carol, emphasising the Christian nature of the story.

How is each stave structured to keep the reader interested?

Stave 1 begins with **exposition**. First, Dickens tells us about Scrooge and describes a series of encounters with other characters, which show his character and attitudes. There is a change in mood when Marley's ghost appears. Marley's warning to Scrooge and the information that three spirits will visit him build up the reader's interest in what might happen next.

Stave 2 consists of a series of scenes where the Ghost of Christmas Past takes Scrooge to see events from his past. These are a bit like **flashbacks**. They are ordered **chronologically** and tell us Scrooge's history. Each scene causes an emotional reaction in Scrooge. A reader's reactions might follow Scrooge's: pity; hope; happiness; regret; and shame. The end of this stave leaves us wondering if Scrooge can be saved.

Stave 3 follows a similar pattern as the Ghost of Christmas Present shows Scrooge scenes of people enjoying Christmas in the present day. It gives a general picture of people across the country and more detailed accounts of Christmas at the Cratchits' house and at Fred's house. From each scene, Scrooge gains a better understanding of the meaning of Christmas. However, this stave ends with a twist as the Ghost reveals Ignorance and Want. This shocks Scrooge and the reader into thinking about social issues and how we should respond to them.

In Stave 4 the mood becomes darker as the Ghost of Christmas Yet to Come shows Scrooge several disturbing scenes. Dickens builds a sense of mystery by not having the Ghost explain anything. We might, like Scrooge, wonder who the dead man is. We might be shocked by the revelation that Tiny Tim is dead. The stave ends in a **cliffhanger** as the Ghost does not answer Scrooge's question; can he change the future?

Stave 5 brings us back to Scrooge's bedroom on Christmas morning. He is relieved to see that the 'future' events that he saw have not taken place. Scrooge has been saved by the spirits and the story ends with Dickens telling us about how Scrooge's life changes and the effect of this on others, leaving us to draw a moral lesson from the story.

Key Quotations to Learn

Marley was dead, to begin with. (Stave 1)

The Phantom slowly, gravely, silently approached. (Stave 4)

And so, as Tiny Tim observed, 'God bless Us, Every One!' (Stave 4)

Summary

- Dickens divides the story into 'staves' to reinforce the idea that it is a Christmas carol in prose.
- The first stave is mostly exposition, telling us about Scrooge.
- Staves 2, 3 and 4 contain a series of scenes shown to Scrooge by the Ghosts.
- The final stave shows us the new Scrooge, his actions contrasting with his actions in Stave 1.

Questions

QUICK TEST
1. Why does Dickens call the chapters 'staves'?
2. In what order does Dickens show the events of Scrooge's past?
3. How does Dickens suddenly change the mood at the end of Stave 3?
4. How does Dickens create an air of mystery in Stave 4?

EXAM PRACTICE
Using one or more of the 'Key Quotations to Learn', write a paragraph analysing how Dickens uses structure to involve the reader in the novel.

Why did Charles Dickens write *A Christmas Carol*?

You must be able to: understand how the novel's meaning has been shaped by the author's life and his reasons for writing the novel.

Who was Charles Dickens?

Charles Dickens was born in 1812 in Portsmouth, Hampshire.

His family was middle-class but his father lost his money and he had to go to a **debtors' prison**. As a child, Dickens had to work in a factory. These experiences deeply affected him.

Although he did not have much formal education, Dickens became a journalist and editor.

He published his first novel, *The Pickwick Papers*, in 1836. He soon became one of the most popular and successful novelists in Britain and the world.

He had ten children with his wife, Catherine, but the marriage was not always happy and they separated. However, this did not alter his belief in family life.

He loved parties and would put on plays and entertainment for his family and friends.

He campaigned throughout his life on issues of **social reform**, such as children's issues, and those affecting women, particularly 'fallen' women.

He died in 1870.

Why did he write *A Christmas Carol*?

In 1843, Dickens read a government report on child labour in England. The report was based on interviews that a journalist had done with children about their work. Their stories are reflected in characters such as Martha Cratchit, who works long hours making hats for rich people.

He wanted to use his popularity to bring the problem of child poverty to the attention of a wider public. His first idea was to write a pamphlet called 'An Appeal to the People of England on behalf of the Poor Man's Child'.

He soon realised that an entertaining story would have much more influence. Dickens decided to use a ghost story, which was a popular form at the time.

Why Christmas?

Some people say Dickens 'invented' Christmas. While this is an exaggeration, his work did promote its celebration. He was writing at a time when old Christmas **traditions** were being revived and some new ones introduced. For example, Prince Albert, the husband of Queen Victoria, had recently introduced the Christmas tree from Germany.

A Christmas Carol itself became part of Christmas tradition. Dickens was able to use the fact that Christmas is traditionally a time for giving to remind people of Christian teaching about caring for others and helping the poor.

Summary

- Dickens's early life gave him first-hand experiences of poverty.
- He was a family man who loved celebrations and entertainment.
- He was very concerned about poverty, especially how it affected children.
- He used his popularity as a writer and people's love of Christmas to put across his message in *A Christmas Carol*.

Questions

QUICK TEST
1. What childhood experiences influenced Dickens's feelings about poverty?
2. What made Dickens want to write a pamphlet about poor children?
3. Which character was inspired by accounts of children working long hours?

EXAM PRACTICE
And Martha, who was a poor apprentice at a **milliner's**, then told them what kind of work she had to do, and how many hours she worked at a stretch, and how she meant to lie a-bed tomorrow morning for a good long rest; tomorrow being a holiday she passed at home. (Stave 3)

Relating your ideas to the historical context, write a paragraph explaining how Dickens portrays children in *A Christmas Carol*.

The Setting of *A Christmas Carol*

You must be able to: understand how the novel's setting reflects the themes of the novel.

Where is it set?

It is set mostly in London but briefly in other parts of Britain.

What was Victorian London like?

London was the capital of the United Kingdom and of the British Empire. In 1841, it had a population of nearly two million, making it the largest city in the world.

It was the centre of government, business and finance as well as being the empire's largest port. It was a very wealthy city but many people were extremely poor.

The city was very unhealthy, with no sewers until 1870, and diseases such as cholera were common.

How is London portrayed in the novel?

The main action takes place in the city of London, the centre of business, where Scrooge has his counting house. The rooms where Scrooge lives are described as 'gloomy', reflecting his character.

In Stave 4 the Ghost of Christmas Yet to Come takes Scrooge to the 'Change (Exchange), a place where business deals were done. Here Scrooge sees wealthy businessmen chatting about his death.

In contrast, Scrooge is then taken to a shop in a part of town where the 'ways were foul and narrow'. Here he sees three characters sell the things they have stolen from the dead man.

Dickens's description of the streets of London at Christmas in Stave 5 sum up his feelings about the city. The unpleasant weather is contrasted with the light and colour of the shops. The long lists of produce convey a sense of wonder. Descriptions of people shopping, going to church and collecting their dinners from the bakers' ovens give a sense of the bustling excitement of the city.

Dickens's London can be dangerous and depressing but it is also exciting and full of life.

How are other places portrayed in the novel?

The Ghost of Christmas Past and the Ghost of Christmas Present both briefly take Scrooge out of London.

The school Scrooge attended as a boy is isolated, run down and lonely. Dickens uses **pathetic fallacy**, his descriptions of 'the melancholy room' and 'the despondent poplar' reflecting the young Scrooge's loneliness.

The Ghost of Christmas Present shows Scrooge a variety of places. The landscapes are harsh and people struggle to live there: the 'bleak and desert moor' where the miners live; the frightful range of rocks' where the lighthouse is; and 'the black and heaving sea' where they see the sailors.

In each of these passages, nature is hostile and survival difficult, but the men and women who live and work there still joyfully celebrate Christmas.

Key Quotations to Learn

A bare melancholy room. (Stave 1)

There was nothing very cheerful in the climate of the town, and yet there was an air of cheerfulness abroad. (Stave 3)

The whole quarter reeked with crime, with filth and misery. (Stave 4)

Summary

- London was a city of great wealth and great poverty.
- Dickens writes about both the hardships and the excitement of living in the city.
- The descriptions of Scrooge's home and his old school reflect his feelings and character.
- The other places he describes are harsh and dangerous.

Questions

QUICK TEST
1. Where is Scrooge's counting house?
2. In London, what contrasts with the dull, gloomy weather?
3. Which three places outside London does the Ghost of Christmas Present show to Scrooge?

EXAM PRACTICE
Using at least one of the 'Key Quotations to Learn', explain how Dickens uses a description of a place to create mood and atmosphere.

Social Class and Gender

You must be able to: understand the importance of social class and gender in Victorian times and their role in the novel.

What is meant by class?

Class is a way of grouping different people in society according to their social status and wealth.

How are different social classes shown in the novel?

Upper-class people belong to old, established families that own a lot of land and property. There are no upper-class characters in the novel.

The 'middle class' includes businessmen and 'professionals' such as lawyers, doctors and teachers. They might be well-educated, own their own homes and have servants. Scrooge, Fred, Fezziwig, the businessmen at the 'Change and the portly gentlemen are middle class.

The Cratchits are described as 'poor' so might be thought of as working class. However, working class people are traditionally those who do manual labour. Bob works in an office and must have a reasonable level of education to do his job. Someone like him might have been referred to as 'lower middle-class' or '**respectable** working class'.

Those who do work with their hands include the miners, the sailors, the charwoman and laundress. In the nineteenth century a lot of work was casual, there was little protection for workers and there were no welfare benefits. It was easy to fall from being a 'respectable' working man or woman to being a beggar or petty criminal. Poverty and starvation were never far away.

What is meant by gender roles?

At different times and in different places, men and women are expected to play different parts in society.

In Victorian society, men had more rights than women. For example, women could not vote in elections (though most men could not either) and married women could not own property (until 1882).

Victorian society saw women as being wives and mothers. When married, they were expected to obey their husbands. In return, men were expected to provide for their wives.

How are gender roles presented in the novel?

Mrs Cratchit is a wife and mother. Her job is looking after the house and children; not just cleaning and cooking but also making the family's money stretch as far as it can, for example, by repairing old clothes. She is seen as a 'good wife'.

Belle too becomes a model wife, devoting herself to her many children. However, when she is young, she is in a very precarious position. She has no **dowry** to bring to a marriage with Scrooge. A middle-class girl without money might have trouble finding a husband.

Younger middle-class women such as Fezziwig's daughters and Fred's sister-in-law are seen in terms of their romantic prospects. Pretty and lively, they should have no trouble finding husbands.

Other women work for a living. The charwoman and laundress are in badly paid casual work and resort to stealing from the dead. Martha Cratchit is also poorly paid but she has an apprenticeship: millinery is skilled work and she should be able to contribute to the family expenses until she marries.

Summary

- Dickens includes a range of middle-class and working-class characters in the novel.
- Finding and keeping work was difficult for working-class people.
- Men and women were expected to play different roles in Victorian society.
- The married women in *A Christmas Carol* are seen as good wives and mothers.

Questions

QUICK TEST
1. To what social class does Mr Fezziwig belong?
2. Give three examples of paid work done by women in the novel.
3. Name two things that women could not do when *A Christmas Carol* was written.
4. Name two mothers in *A Christmas Carol*.

EXAM PRACTICE
Relating your ideas to the historical context, write a paragraph explaining what is meant by a 'good wife' in *A Christmas Carol*.

The Poor

You must be able to: understand Victorian attitudes to the poor and how these are reflected in *A Christmas Carol*.

Who were the poor?

Dickens wanted to write about the children of the poor, but who were the poor? As a result of **industrialisation**, there were many people in Victorian Britain who earned little or nothing, while living and working in terrible conditions. Many children were sent to work in dangerous badly paid jobs while others roamed the streets because their parents could not afford to keep them. But 'rich' and 'poor' are comparative terms and in *A Christmas Carol* many people are described as poor.

How are poor people presented in *A Christmas Carol*?

The Cratchits are described as poor, yet compared with many Victorians they are not. Bob earns 15 shillings a week and soon Peter, as well as Martha, will be earning a little. However, they would seem poor to most readers both now and in the nineteenth century. They are shown making the best of the little they have.

Where the Cratchits are poor but honest, the people who visit the shop (Stave 4) are dishonest. They steal to supplement their low income. Poverty and crime were closely linked, as Scrooge implies when he suggests prison as an answer to poverty.

Worse off still are the people who live around the shop. 'Half naked, drunken, slipshod, ugly', they display the effects of extreme poverty.

Want, the **personification** of poverty, confronts us with an **image** of what the poorest in society are like (Stave 3). She is so degraded that she has become more like an animal than human.

What was the workhouse?

Scrooge says the poor should go the workhouses but the portly gentlemen reply that many would rather die.

The workhouse was intended for people who could not support themselves. After the new **Poor Law** was passed in 1834, going there was the only way of getting help. Life there was meant to be harsh so that only the very poor would apply. Inmates worked on tasks such as breaking stones or crushing bones. However, they did receive free medical care and education, which were not available to poor people outside.

What attitudes to the poor are shown in *A Christmas Carol*?

Responses to the problems of poverty varied greatly. Scrooge's assertion that the poor should die to reduce the population reflects the ideas of Thomas Robert Malthus, who had written in 1798 that Britain's 'surplus population' had to be reduced naturally by famine and disease.

On the other hand, the Chartists, a political movement, argued for revolution, something feared by many Victorians. The Ghost of Christmas Present warns of the possibility of revolution.

Some politicians were working to help the poor. The 1844 Factories Act reduced the number of hours 9–13 year olds could work to nine hours a day, six days a week. This may not seem much but it was a great improvement at the time.

Many charities to help the poor were also founded by **philanthropists** and churches, for example, the Ragged School Union, which was founded in 1844 and was supported by Dickens.

Summary

- Poverty was a huge problem, the result of industrialisation and increasing population.
- Children worked long hours in dangerous jobs from an early age.
- The only provision for those who could not work was the workhouse.
- Proposed solutions to the problem of the poor ranged from letting them die to revolution.
- Many charities were founded to help the poor.

Questions

QUICK TEST
1. Give two reasons for the increase in poverty in the nineteenth century.
2. Give two examples of work people might do in the workhouse.
3. What was Malthus's solution to the problem of poverty?
4. What was the Chartists's solution?

EXAM PRACTICE
Relating your ideas to the historical context, write a paragraph about Scrooge's attitude to poverty in Stave 1.

Christianity and Morality

You must be able to: understand how Christian beliefs and morality are reflected in *A Christmas Carol*.

Was Christianity widespread in the nineteenth century?

Britain was an overwhelmingly Christian country. Very few people belonged to non-Christian religions or had no religion. About half the population attended church or chapel regularly.

The **established church** was the Church of England but there were many other **denominations**, including Roman Catholics, Methodists, Baptist and Congregationalists. There were also different strands within the Church of England.

What do Christians believe?

Christians believe that there is one God who made the world and that God sent his son, Jesus Christ, to save us.

Christmas Day is the celebration of Christ's birth in a stable in Bethlehem. His life, his teachings and his death are recorded in the Gospels of the New Testament.

Christians believe that mankind was in a state of **sin** and that Christ's death 'redeemed' us, meaning that our sins can be forgiven and that after death we can join God in Heaven.

Different denominations have different ideas about how people can get to Heaven. Most mainstream Christians believe that we can achieve Heaven by praying and living good lives (faith and works).

What is morality?

Morality is the understanding of right and wrong by which people live their lives. Ideas of morality differ in different societies and can change over the years.

In Victorian Britain, most people's sense of morality was firmly based on the Ten Commandments of the Old Testament and Christ's teaching in the New Testament.

However, all these teachings are open to interpretation. For example, some Christians (sometimes referred to as Puritans) believe that drinking alcohol, dancing and playing games are immoral. The characters of *A Christmas Carol* clearly do not interpret Christian morality in this severe way.

There are also differences about how much we should try to help others. Some people might believe that it is God's will whether people are rich or poor, well or sick, and so they should accept their suffering and be rewarded after death. Most people, however, believe that Christ teaches us to show **compassion** to others and help them in practical ways.

Christian churches and individuals were behind many of the charities and social reform movements of the nineteenth century.

How are Christian beliefs and morals shown in *A Christmas Carol*?

There are references to Christian beliefs and morality throughout the novel.

Scrooge is described as a 'sinner' and his behaviour to others as unchristian.

Fred refers directly to the 'sacred origin' of Christmas and the portly gentlemen appeal for 'Christian cheer'.

Tiny Tim speaks directly of Christ's teachings on his return from church. The family's reaction to his 'death' is rooted in Christian belief.

The whole story is one of redemption as Scrooge is forgiven for his past sins and becomes a new man.

Summary

- Britain was overwhelmingly Christian in the nineteenth century.
- Christmas is the celebration of the birth of Jesus Christ.
- Ideas of right and wrong were rooted in Christian teaching.
- Not all Christians had the same ideas about morality.
- There are frequent references to Christ and Christianity in *A Christmas Carol*.

Questions

QUICK TEST
1. What proportion of people went to church regularly in 1851?
2. How do most Christians believe we can get to Heaven?
3. What do the Fezziwigs and Fred do that Puritans would consider sinful?
4. On what two things were Victorian ideas of morality based?

EXAM PRACTICE
Write a paragraph about how one of the following characters is shown as an example of Christianity:
- Fred
- Mr Fezziwig
- Bob Cratchit.

You must be able to: analyse how Scrooge is presented in the novel.

Who is Scrooge?

Scrooge is a businessman who has an office (or 'counting house') in the City of London.

What is his function in the novel?

Scrooge is the **protagonist** (the main character) of *A Christmas Carol*. The story is about how his experiences change him.

What is his character?

Scrooge is mean, greedy, unsociable and secretive. His character is reflected in his looks. He has a pointed nose, shrivelled cheeks, red eyes, blue lips and white hair. He walks stiffly and speaks in a grating voice.

He hates Christmas.

How do people react to him?

People avoid Scrooge: nobody stops in the street to greet him. Beggars do not beg from him. Nobody asks him the time or asks for directions from him.

His nephew, Fred, tries to be friendly towards him but makes fun of him in a good-natured way.

Mrs Cratchit criticises Scrooge for the way he treats her husband, Bob.

When Scrooge is shown his own death, he sees how little love and respect people have for him. His fellow businessmen do not care. His charwoman, the laundress and the undertaker steal from him. People who owe him money are glad that he is dead.

How does Scrooge behave towards others?

He does not allow his clerk, Bob Cratchit, enough coal for the fire.

He angrily rejects Fred's invitation and criticises him for marrying with no money.

He refuses to help the poor, telling the two portly gentlemen that the poor should either go to the workhouse or die.

He chases away a carol singer.

Was he always like this?

The Ghost of Christmas Past shows Scrooge (and us) how much he has changed.

As a boy, he was lonely, left in a boarding school by his uncaring father. However, he enjoyed reading and loved his sister, Fan.

As a young man, Scrooge enjoyed Christmas and was well-treated by his employer, Mr Fezziwig, at whose party he danced and had fun with his friends.

He was engaged to Belle but she realised he did not want to marry her because he was only interested in money and she had none. We are not told when or why he became like this, except that he is afraid of poverty.

Key Quotations to Learn

The cold within him froze his old features. (Stave 1)

A squeezing, wrenching, grasping, scraping, clutching, covetous old sinner! (Stave 1)

He carried his own low temperature always about with him. (Stave 1)

Summary

- Dickens describes Scrooge in great detail.
- His looks reflect his nature.
- Other people avoid him and nobody (except Fred) cares about him.
- He hates Christmas and does not believe in helping the poor.

Sample Analysis

At the beginning of the novel, Dickens describes Scrooge and how people see him in great detail. He builds up a picture of his character using a series of **adjectives**: squeezing, wrenching, grasping, covetous. The coldness of his nature is compared to the coldness of the winter weather: 'The cold within him froze his old features.' This cold, selfish nature affects all those who come into contact with him so that 'even the blind men's dogs' avoid him.

Questions

QUICK TEST
1. What colour are Scrooge's eyes, lips and hair?
2. Who was Belle?
3. Has Scrooge always hated Christmas? Give a reason for your answer.
4. What is another word for the main character in a novel?

EXAM PRACTICE
Using at least one of the 'Key Quotations to Learn', write a paragraph explaining how Dickens conveys Scrooge's character at the beginning of the novel.

Scrooge (2)

You must be able to: analyse how Scrooge changes in the novel.

How does Scrooge change?

The Ghosts help Scrooge to change for the better.

How does he start to change?

The Ghost of Christmas Past takes Scrooge back in time to see what he used to be like.

When he sees how unhappy he was as a boy, he sheds a tear. This is the first time he shows emotion.

When he sees Mr Fezziwig and remembers what a good employer he was, he thinks of his own clerk, Bob Cratchit. He is beginning to see that there is a better way of treating people.

The Ghost shows him how things have turned out for Belle. She has a loving family when he has no-one. Seeing this upsets Scrooge and he says he cannot bear it.

How does the Ghost of Christmas Present help him to change?

The Ghost of Christmas Present shows Scrooge people enjoying Christmas.

He is moved by watching the Cratchits making the most of the little they have. He is upset by seeing how ill Tiny Tim is, showing sympathy and concern.

Watching the party at his nephew's house, he starts to enjoy himself, joining in with the games and laughter.

Finally, the Ghost shows him Ignorance and Want to help him to change his ideas about poverty.

How does the Ghost of Christmas Yet to Come help him change?

The Ghost shows him what will happen if he does not change his behaviour.

He is shocked and upset to learn that Tiny Tim will die, and he himself will die alone and unloved.

He begs the Ghost to tell him that he can change the future by changing his behaviour. He promises to learn the lessons the Ghosts have taught him.

What is Scrooge like at the end of the novel?

Scrooge changes his behaviour totally. He is generous, helping the Cratchits and giving to the poor. He is reconciled with his nephew and enjoys Christmas and the rest of his life.

Key Quotations to Learn

'Your lip is trembling,' said the Ghost. 'And what is that upon your cheek?' (Stave 2)

Scrooge hung his head to hear his own words quoted by the Spirit, and was overcome with **penitence** and grief. (Stave 3)

'I will honour Christmas in my heart, and try to keep it all the year.' (Scrooge: Stave 5)

Summary

- Scrooge changes because of what the Ghosts show him.
- He starts to feel emotion when he sees his younger self.
- He feels sympathy for Tiny Tim.
- He learns to enjoy himself.
- By the end of the novel, Scrooge has changed completely.

Sample Analysis

Scrooge asks the Ghost of Christmas Present about Tiny Tim's fate 'with an interest he had never felt before'. The Ghost replies by telling him that he sees 'a vacant seat', indicating that Tim will die. When Scrooge protests, the Ghost quotes his own words back at him: 'If he be like to die, he had better do it, and decrease the surplus population'. Hearing this, Scrooge is 'overcome with penitence and grief', marking a great change in his character as he shows a selfless interest in another person and recognises his previous selfishness and lack of care.

Questions

QUICK TEST
1. What makes Scrooge cry?
2. What is his reaction to seeing Belle's family?
3. How does he hope to alter the future?
4. Which three of the following adjectives describe Scrooge at the end of the novel?
   spiteful; generous; happy; cruel; mean; popular.

EXAM PRACTICE
Using at least one of the 'Key Quotations to Learn', write a paragraph explaining how Scrooge's character has changed by the end of the novel.

Marley's Ghost and The Ghost of Christmas Past

You must be able to: analyse the characters of Marley's Ghost and the Ghost of Christmas Past and their function in the novel.

Who is/was Marley?

The first sentence of the novel is 'Marley was dead, to begin with'. Marley was Scrooge's business partner and perhaps his only friend. He died seven years before the start of the story. In Stave 1, Marley's ghost appears to Scrooge.

What is his character?

Marley appears the same as he did in life; but his jaw is bound up, he drags a long chain behind him and he is transparent.

His sudden appearance, the cries he makes and the clanking of his chain make him a terrifying vision.

In life, he was very much like Scrooge. In death, he has been condemned to travel the world, tortured by remorse for his behaviour in life.

What is his function in the novel?

Marley visits Scrooge to show what might happen if he does not change his behaviour.

He warns Scrooge that he must change and tells him that he will have three visits from spirits.

Scrooge's reaction to him also provides some humour.

What is the Ghost of Christmas Past?

It is the first of the three spirits. It represents all the Christmases that have gone before.

What is its character?

It is a strange figure, part child, part old man. It has white hair but a young face. It has long muscular arms and hands but delicate legs and feet. It wears a white tunic, trimmed with flowers and with a glittering belt. It carries a sprig of holly.

From its head springs a jet of light. It carries a white cap that can be used to extinguish the light.

It is usually gentle and encouraging towards Scrooge but can also be forceful, physically forcing him to watch Belle and her family.

What is its function in the novel?

The Ghost of Christmas Past shows Scrooge Christmases from his past, showing him how he has changed and helping him to experience feelings, both happy and sad.

At the beginning of the Stave, Scrooge wants the Ghost to cover its light, which symbolises knowledge and understanding. At the end of the Stave, when this light burns brightly, Scrooge forces the cap onto the Ghost but cannot put out the light completely.

Key Quotations to Learn

'I wear the chain I forged in life', replied the Ghost. (Stave 1)

'Mankind was my business.' (Marley's Ghost: Stave 1)

'No, Your past.' (The Ghost of Christmas Past: Stave 2)

Summary

- Marley was Scrooge's business partner.
- He is weighed down by a chain symbolising his badly spent life.
- He warns Scrooge that he must change.
- The Ghost of Christmas Past shows Scrooge his past, causing a mixture of emotions.
- A bright light springs from the Ghost's head.

Sample Analysis

Marley's chain is made up of 'cash boxes, keys, padlocks, **ledgers**, **deeds**, and heavy purses wrought in steel'. This long list of items is associated with money and business, showing what was important to Marley in life. His earthly attachment to these **symbols** of greed is the reason that after death he can have no peace.

Questions

QUICK TEST
1. Name three things that make up Marley's chain.
2. What has Marley been condemned to do?
3. What two things does the Ghost of Christmas Past carry?
4. What does Scrooge do to the Ghost at the end of the Stave?

EXAM PRACTICE
Using at least one of the 'Key Quotations to Learn', write a paragraph about the Ghost of Christmas Past, explaining what it represents and how it helps Scrooge.

The Ghost of Christmas Present and The Ghost of Christmas Yet to Come

You must be able to: analyse the characters of the Ghosts and their function in the novel.

What is the Ghost of Christmas Present?

It is the second of the three spirits that visit Scrooge. It represents the present Christmas season.

What is its character?

When Scrooge first sees the Ghost of Christmas Present, it is surrounded by Christmas decorations and piles of food, on which it sits as on a throne. It is a 'jolly giant, wearing a green robe trimmed with white fur'. On its head is a holly wreath. It has long dark curly hair and a 'sparkling eye'.

This Ghost is cheerful and kind. It carries a burning torch from which it casts incense on people's dinners. When it casts the incense on people, they stop quarrelling.

This Ghost is sometimes severe, rebuking Scrooge and reminding him of things he has said.

It only lives for **the twelve days of Christmas**, towards the end of which it grows older.

What is its function in the novel?

The Ghost of Christmas Present shows Scrooge how others celebrate the true spirit of Christmas: enjoyment, love and caring for others.

It helps Scrooge to see that money is not everything and that everyone, however poor, can enjoy Christmas.

It also enables him to see the happiness that family life can bring.

Finally, it shows Scrooge the monstrous children, Ignorance and Want, a terrible warning about what could happen if the problems of society are not addressed.

What is the Ghost of Christmas Yet to Come?

The Ghost of Christmas Yet to Come is the third of the three spirits. It represents the future.

What is its character?

The appearance of the Ghost of Christmas Yet to Come is reminiscent of the personification of Death. It is covered in a long black cloak. Its face cannot be seen. From the cloak emerges one outstretched hand. It is slow, stately and solemn.

This Ghost does not speak but points at things and lets Scrooge come to his own conclusions.

What is its function in the novel?

This Ghost gives Scrooge a vision of what the future might hold. This vision upsets and frightens Scrooge, so that he finally promises to change.

Key Quotations to Learn

In easy state upon this couch there sat a jolly Giant, glorious to see. (Stave 3)

... its genial face, its sparkling eye, its open hand, its cheery voice, its unconstrained demeanour, and its joyful air. (Stave 3)

The Spirit was immovable as ever. (Stave 4)

Summary

- The Ghost of Christmas Present shows Scrooge how others celebrate Christmas.
- It spreads kindness and joy through its torch.
- The Ghost of Christmas Yet to Come is dark, gloomy and mysterious.
- It shows Scrooge how things might turn out, causing him to change his ways.

Sample Analysis

The Ghost casts 'incense' from its torch on the dinners that people have collected from the baker's, somehow transforming what these 'poor revellers' are about to eat. The torch has previously been described as being 'not unlike Plenty's horn'. Its incense also has the effect of stopping quarrels. We can infer that two aspects of the Christmas spirit are united in it: peace and **plenty**.

Questions

QUICK TEST
1. What does the Ghost of Christmas Present do with its torch?
2. How long does it live?
3. What does it wear?
4. What is the only part of the Ghost of Christmas Yet to Come that Scrooge can see?

EXAM PRACTICE
Using at least one of the 'Key Quotations to Learn', write one paragraph about the Ghost of Christmas Present and one about the Ghost of Christmas Yet to Come, explaining what they represent and the effect they have on Scrooge.

You must be able to: analyse the characters of the Cratchit family.

Who are the Cratchits?

Bob Cratchit is Scrooge's clerk at the counting-house. He lives with his wife and children: Martha, Peter, 'Tiny' Tim, Belinda and two 'young Cratchits'.

What is Bob's character?

He is hard-working and, although not well treated by Scrooge, he does not complain.

He is good-natured and cheerful. He enjoys Christmas, making the most of what he can afford.

He is a loving and caring father. He is devoted to Tiny Tim and he praises his wife for what she does for the family.

He is sensitive and gentle. He gets upset about Tiny Tim and he even refuses to criticise Scrooge, telling off his wife for wanting to give him a 'piece of [her] mind'.

What is Bob's function in the novel?

Through Bob, we see how Scrooge treats people. He is not allowed coal for the fire in his office. He only gets one day off for Christmas. He is badly paid.

The Cratchits are typical of many people at the time. They are not the poorest in society but they struggle to make ends meet. Their clothes and shoes are worn and they have few possessions.

Despite this, Bob and his family are happy and loving. Scrooge learns from them that money is not everything.

What is Tiny Tim's character?

He is small and delicate, using crutches to walk. He is obviously very ill but we are not told what is wrong with him.

He is very close to his father. Tim thinks that seeing him in church might remind people of what Jesus said about making the **lame** walk and the blind see.

Bob describes him as 'patient' and 'mild'.

In Stave 4, we see the effect of his death in a passage of great **pathos**.

What is Tiny Tim's function in the novel?

It is Tiny Tim who really makes Scrooge think about others. His situation makes Scrooge realise the reality of poverty and that many who are suffering could be helped.

Key Quotations to Learn

'My dear!' was Bob's mild answer. 'Christmas day!' (Stave 3)

'I see a vacant seat,' replied the Ghost, 'in the poor chimney-corner, and a crutch without an owner, carefully preserved.' (Stave 3)

... and to Tiny Tim, who did NOT die, he was a second father. (Stave 5)

Summary

- Bob Cratchit is Scrooge's clerk and is treated badly by him.
- The Cratchits are poor but they love Christmas and celebrate it well, remembering its true meaning.
- Seeing Tiny Tim teaches Scrooge about the reality of poverty and illness.
- The Cratchits help Scrooge to change. He becomes a good employer and a friend to the family.

Sample Analysis

Mrs Cratchit reacts angrily to her husband proposing a toast to Scrooge as 'Founder of the Feast'. Her honest description of him as an 'odious, stingy, hard, unfeeling' man reflects what we already know about him, though it is the first time that Scrooge himself has heard it. Bob's mild answer is simply that it is 'Christmas-day'. This shows the difference in their characters, implying that he does not disagree but that he believes strongly in Christmas as a time of goodwill to all men, however 'odious'.

Questions

QUICK TEST
1. Name four of Bob Cratchit's children.
2. How do Mr and Mrs Cratchit differ in their attitude to Scrooge?
3. Why does Tim hope that people saw him in church?
4. What two words does Bob use about Tiny Tim?

EXAM PRACTICE
Using at least one of the 'Key Quotations to Learn', write a paragraph about the Cratchit family, explaining what they represent and the effect they have on Scrooge.

Fred and Fan

You must be able to: analyse the characters of Fred and Fan and their importance in the novel.

Who is Fred?

Fred is Scrooge's nephew, the son of Scrooge's sister, Fan. He has recently married.

What is Fred's character?

In contrast to Scrooge, Fred is happy, outgoing and generous.

He values love over money. Fred has married despite Scrooge saying he cannot afford to.

He enjoys entertaining his friends and playing games.

He makes fun of Scrooge but is not nasty or malicious. Fred is not concerned or provoked by Scrooge's attitude to him.

What is his function in the novel?

He forms a contrast to Scrooge. He has married for love, whereas Scrooge chose money over love. He is very sociable and loves Christmas, whereas Scrooge is solitary and hates Christmas.

He gives his view about Christmas: how the celebrations make people think of others and how this spirit is connected to its religious **significance**. This reflects Dickens's own view.

His Christmas party shows a typical middle-class celebration of Christmas. Fred's family and friends are younger and better-off than the Cratchits but they too have the spirit of Christmas.

Who is Fan?

Fan is Scrooge's sister and Fred's mother. She has died before the novel begins.

What is her character?

She is gentle and loving.

She is cheerful and looks forward enthusiastically to Christmas with Scrooge.

What is her function in the novel?

Through her, we see a different side of Scrooge: that when he was young, he was loved by someone and he loved her in return.

We also see that the family was not always happy, but when she comes to collect Scrooge from school she tells him that things are much better at home.

Being reminded of her early death, Scrooge thinks about Fred and is 'uneasy in his mind'.

Key Quotations to Learn

'Why did you get married?' said Scrooge.
'Because I fell in love.' (Fred: Stave 1)

'I am sorry for him; I couldn't be angry with him if I tried. Who suffers by his ill whims? Himself always.' (Fred: Stave 3)

'Always a delicate creature … But she had a large heart!'
(The Ghost of Christmas Past: Stave 2)

Summary

- Fred is Scrooge's nephew, his sister's son.
- He gives Dickens's view of Christmas.
- His character forms a contrast with Scrooge.
- His party shows young people enjoying Christmas.
- Fan and Scrooge loved each other but their family was not a happy one.

Sample Analysis

Dickens does not tell us much about the young Scrooge's family life but Fan's description of it now being 'like Heaven' and her delight that her father 'is so much kinder than he used to be' suggest that he has been unloving in the past. This idea is supported by the way that until now he has left Scrooge at school over Christmas. The fact that Fan only mentions her father implies that their mother is dead, perhaps explaining the father's mood. These hints, together with Fan's own early death, help the reader to become more sympathetic towards the adult Scrooge.

Questions

QUICK TEST
1. What has Fred recently done that Scrooge disapproves of?
2. Give two ways in which Fred is the opposite of Scrooge.
3. What effect does Fred think Christmas has on people?
4. What does Fan tell Scrooge when she collects him from school?

EXAM PRACTICE
Using at least one of the 'Key Quotations to Learn', write a paragraph about Fred, explaining his character and his relationship with Scrooge.

Mr Fezziwig and Belle

You must be able to: analyse the characters of Mr Fezziwig and Belle and their importance in the novel.

Who is Mr Fezziwig?

Mr Fezziwig was Scrooge's employer when he was a young clerk. The Ghost of Christmas Past shows Scrooge Mr Fezziwig's Christmas party.

What is Mr Fezziwig's character?

He is 'an old gentleman in a Welsh wig'. He is jovial with a rich voice. When he walks, he skips.

He is fair to his employees, treating them well.

He is generous with his money, throwing a big Christmas party.

He has a happy family life with his wife and daughters. He and his wife love dancing and are the life and soul of the party.

What is his function in the novel?

He forms a contrast to Scrooge. His behaviour towards young Scrooge and his fellow clerk and friend, Dick Wilkins, is the opposite of old Scrooge's treatment of Bob Cratchit.

Unlike Scrooge, he celebrates Christmas by not only enjoying himself but by making sure his family, friends and employees enjoy themselves too.

Who is Belle?

Belle was Scrooge's fiancée. The Ghost of Christmas Past shows Belle releasing Scrooge from their engagement and, later, when she is married to someone else.

What is her character?

When we first see Belle, she is in mourning, so we can **infer** that her parents or guardians have recently died.

Her bereavement has left her poor. She is gentle but straightforward and honest.

She becomes a 'comely matron', playing and laughing with her children.

What is her function in the novel?

Through Belle, we see how Scrooge has changed from the time when he worked for Fezziwig.

We can see how Scrooge has been in love but has lost the chance of happiness through his love of money.

Belle's happy marriage contrasts with Scrooge and seeing her husband and children makes him realise what he has missed.

Key Quotations to Learn

'The happiness he gives is quite as great as if it cost a fortune.' (Scrooge: Stave 2)

... a fair young girl in a mourning dress ... (Stave 2)

'Another **Idol** has displaced me ...' (Belle: Stave 2)

Summary

- Scrooge is Mr Fezziwig's clerk.
- Fezziwig's treatment of his employees contrasts with Scrooge's treatment of Bob Cratchit.
- His generosity and enjoyment of Christmas also contrast with Scrooge.
- Belle releases Scrooge from their engagement because she knows he loves money more than he loves her.
- In contrast to Scrooge, Belle has children and a happy marriage.

Sample Analysis

The scene where Scrooge and the Ghost of Christmas Past watch Belle's family gives a glimpse of family life that forms a stark contrast with Scrooge's life. Adjectives such as 'tumultuous' and 'uproarious' and the phrase 'pillaged by the brigands most ruthlessly' could paint a violent, dangerous picture but they are put into context by the observation that 'the mother and daughter laughed heartily'. It is a playful and chaotic scene reflecting spontaneous enjoyment, which is in keeping with Dickens's idea of Christmas.

Questions

QUICK TEST
1. What is Fezziwig's relationship with Scrooge?
2. What does Fezziwig do to make his employees and friends happy?
3. Why does Belle think Scrooge will not want to marry her?
4. How does Belle's later life contrast with Scrooge's?

EXAM PRACTICE
Using at least one of the 'Key Quotations to Learn', write a paragraph about Belle, explaining her character and her importance to the story.

The Spirit of Christmas

You must be able to: understand what is meant by the 'spirit of Christmas' and analyse how it is presented in the novel.

What is the spirit of Christmas?

Dickens refers to the spirit of Christmas, honouring Christmas and keeping Christmas well.

Fred sums up the spirit of Christmas in Stave 1. He describes it as a time when people 'seem by one consent to open their shut-up hearts freely'.

In the novel, Christmas is described in terms of religion, tradition and selfless behaviour.

How is the spirit of Christmas represented symbolically?

The Ghost of Christmas Present provides an image of the spirit of Christmas. It is surrounded by things associated with Christmas. Its sword is rusty, suggesting there is no conflict at Christmas. Adjectives such as 'jolly', 'genial' and 'cheery' are used to describe this Ghost.

It uses its torch to spread a mysterious incense, which creates harmony and enjoyment.

What Christmas traditions are shown?

The Ghosts of Christmas Past and Christmas Present are associated with holly. Christmas Present also has ivy and mistletoe. The tradition of bringing these plants indoors at this time of year goes back to pagan festivals.

It is also traditional to feast on food and drink. In the nineteenth century, turkey was replacing goose as the luxury meat for Christmas. Dickens also mentions plum puddings, chestnuts and mince pies.

How is the religious side of Christmas shown?

People, including Bob Cratchit and Tiny Tim, go to church on Christmas morning. Scrooge himself attends church in Stave 5.

Christmas carols are hymns about the birth of Jesus. In Stave 1, a carol singer comes to Scrooge's counting house. In Stave 3, the old miner sings a 'Christmas song' and the sailors hum Christmas tunes.

How do characters honour Christmas in other ways?

The portly gentlemen honour Christmas by collecting for charity.

Fred and Mr Fezziwig throw parties, displaying a spirit of generosity.

Bob Cratchit and Fred show the Christmas spirit in their attitudes towards Scrooge.

In Stave 3, people in the streets, lighthouse men and sailors show Christmas spirit in their good humour and kindness to each other.

Key Quotations to Learn

'... a kind, forgiving, charitable, pleasant time ...' (Fred: Stave 1)

... he spread a few drops of water on them from it, and their good-humour was restored directly. (Stave 3)

'I will honour Christmas in my heart and try to keep it all the year.' (Scrooge: Stave 4)

Summary

- The spirit of Christmas is a combination of religion, enjoyment and charity.
- It is shown symbolically in the Ghost of Christmas Present.
- There are many references to Christmas traditions.
- References to church-going and Christmas carols link the celebrations to religion.
- Characters show the spirit of Christmas in the way they behave towards others.

Sample Analysis

Fred sets out a clear idea of what Christmas should mean. He refers to 'its sacred name and origin', reminding Scrooge that it is the celebration of the birth of Christ, and asserts that nothing about Christmas can be 'apart from that'. This implies that parties and celebrations are not sinful or unchristian but are a way of honouring Christ. He then says that the season encourages people to think of 'people below them', which is exactly what Scrooge does not do when he argues with the charity collectors.

Questions

QUICK TEST
1. Which of the Ghosts symbolises the spirit of Christmas?
2. How does it spread the spirit of Christmas?
3. How do the portly gentlemen show Christmas spirit?
4. How does Mr Fezziwig show Christmas spirit?

EXAM PRACTICE
Using at least one of the 'Key Quotations to Learn', write a paragraph explaining how one or more characters honour the spirit of Christmas.

Money and Avarice

You must be able to: analyse how the themes of money and avarice are presented in the novel.

What is avarice?

Avarice (or Greed) is one of the seven deadly sins of Christian tradition. It is defined as an excessive desire for wealth.

How is money presented in *A Christmas Carol*?

Scrooge is described as a rich man but he does not live like a rich man. He lives in a 'gloomy suite of rooms, consisting of a bedroom, a sitting room and a lumber room'. He eats alone in the same 'melancholy' tavern every night and seems to do nothing except read the papers and do his accounts.

In contrast, Mr Fezziwig shares his wealth and the 'portly gentlemen' collect money to help others.

Scrooge describes Fred as 'poor' but he has a comfortable life and spends his money on Christmas festivities.

The Cratchits do not have much money but they too spend what they have on celebrating Christmas.

There is no sense in the novel that money is always a bad thing. It is people's attitude to money and what they do with it that matters. Scrooge is presented as a miser, someone who hoards wealth and lives miserably.

How is avarice presented?

Scrooge's desire for money makes him mean, as shown in his treatment of Bob Cratchit, and even cruel. This is shown in Stave 4 when Caroline and her husband, who owe him money, are pleased by his 'death' because they cannot imagine anyone else being as 'merciless' as Scrooge.

In Stave 2, Belle tells Scrooge that he has made an 'idol' out of money. His avarice makes him incapable of love as he would always 'weigh everything by Gain'.

Avarice is not just a sin of the rich. In Stave 4, Old Joe, the shopkeeper, and the people selling him stolen goods are also shown to be guilty of avarice. They may not gain as much from their greed as Scrooge, but they are just like him in their attitude. It is fitting that their avarice is fed by stealing from avaricious Scrooge.

Key Quotations to Learn

Oh! But he was a tight-fisted hand at the grindstone, Scrooge! (Stave 1)

'I have seen your nobler aspirations fall off one by one, until the master passion, Gain, engrosses you.' (Belle: Stave 2)

'What Idol has displaced you?' he re-joined.
'A golden one.' (Scrooge/Belle: Stave 2)

Summary

- Scrooge is a rich man but does not live like one.
- Other characters have less money but are generous and enjoy what they have.
- Scrooge's love of money makes him unable to love.
- The people in the shop in Stave 4 are also avaricious.

Sample Analysis

Belle accuses Scrooge of worshipping money by saying that 'another idol has displaced' her. An idol is a false god and the use of the adjective 'golden' makes it clear that she means wealth. However, she is not criticising him for making money. She speaks of them both wanting to 'improve our worldly fortune' by 'patient industry'. This implies that Scrooge has not made his money by honest hard work. It is his worship of money, putting it before everything else, that has corrupted him.

Questions

QUICK TEST
1. What is avarice?
2. Is wealth presented as a bad thing in *A Christmas Carol*?
3. What is a miser?
4. What is the idol that has replaced Belle for Scrooge?

EXAM PRACTICE
Using at least one of the 'Key Quotations to Learn', write a paragraph explaining how avarice is presented in *A Christmas Carol*.

Ignorance and Want

You must be able to: analyse how the themes of ignorance and want are presented in the novel.

What are ignorance and want?

Ignorance is lack of knowledge or education.

Want is another word for need or poverty.

How are Ignorance and Want presented in *A Christmas Carol*?

Ignorance and Want are personified as a boy and a girl who emerge from under The Ghost of Christmas Present's robes.

Their shocking appearance, coming not long after the party at Fred's house, suddenly changes the mood of the novel.

They are hostile but at the same time humble. They are described as monsters, yet their appearance is like that of the many starving children in British cities in the 1840s.

Why are they depicted as children?

Many Victorians, including Dickens, idealised children, seeing them as **innocent**, and were concerned about their suffering.

Ignorance and Want are contrasted with the ideal Victorian child. Instead of displaying 'graceful youth', they look old. Instead of being angels, they are possessed by devils.

By making them children, Dickens shows that these problems particularly affect children. Showing them as children is more shocking and likely to gain sympathy.

What is the cause of ignorance and want?

The Ghost states that they are 'Man's', meaning that they are the result of human actions. This implies that their existence is not inevitable.

Ignorance and want are part of the same problem. Free compulsory education was not introduced until 1870. Until then, most poor children in cities received no education at all.

What does the Ghost's warning mean?

The Ghost tells Scrooge to beware of both children, but especially the boy, who has 'Doom' written on his forehead. This suggests that ignorance could result in the destruction of society, probably by revolution.

The Ghost does not give a solution to the problems of ignorance and want, but reminds Scrooge of his own words about workhouses and prisons. These are obviously not the answer, but what is?

Key Quotations to Learn

Yellow, meagre, ragged, scowling, wolfish; but prostrate, too, in their humility. (Stave 4)

Where angels might have sat enthroned, devils lurked, and glared out menacingly. (Stave 4)

'... on his brow I see that written which is Doom,' (The Ghost of Christmas Present: Stave 4)

Summary

- Ignorance and Want personify lack of education and poverty.
- They are presented as monstrous children.
- They form a contrast with the Victorian ideal of childhood.
- They are the result of mankind's actions.
- If ignorance is not dealt with, society will be destroyed.

Sample Analysis

The **simple sentence** at the start of the paragraph, 'They were a boy and a girl', does not prepare the reader for what is to come – an **emotive** description of two creatures that are the opposite of what we expect from children. The lack of a **verb** in the following **minor sentence** adds to its stark impact. A series of adjectives builds a picture of horror, describing both their physical appearance ('Yellow, meagre') and their nature ('scowling, wolfish'). Then, the second half of the sentence surprises the reader with the contradictory information that they are 'prostrate [...] in their humility'.

Questions

QUICK TEST
1. From where do the children emerge?
2. Give two ways in which they are the opposite of what might be expected of children.
3. Who is responsible for their existence?
4. What is written on Ignorance's brow?

EXAM PRACTICE
Using at least one of the 'Key Quotations to Learn', write a paragraph exploring how Ignorance and Want are presented in *A Christmas Carol*.

Families

You must be able to: analyse how families are presented in the novel.

What families are we shown in *A Christmas Carol*?

There are three families consisting of father, mother and children: the Cratchits, Belle's family and Caroline's family.

Mr and Mrs Fezziwig are shown with their three daughters.

There is a glimpse of a large extended family on the moors.

In the present, Scrooge's nephew Fred is starting family life with his new wife, entertaining her family and their friends.

Scrooge's sister, Fred's mother, is shown to him by the Ghost of Christmas Past, and their father is mentioned.

Love, both love between parents and children and between married couples, is shown within families.

At the end of the novel, Scrooge is welcomed into Fred's family.

How are marriage and family life presented in the novel?

Scrooge is described as 'solitary' and he rejects the invitation of the one family member he has left.

His solitariness is contrasted with the happy families he is shown. The contrast is especially telling at Christmas, traditionally seen as a time for families and children.

Large families are **idealised** in *A Christmas Carol*. When describing Belle's family, Dickens, as an **intrusive narrator**, tells us how he would love to be part of her family. The family is centred on the children, who are playful and noisy, but there are no real tensions or disagreements.

The same is true of the Cratchit children, who are shown helping their parents, joking with them and appreciating what they have done for them. They support each other when Tiny Tim dies in Stave 4.

The presence of four generations at the miner's hut in Stave 3 shows the importance of caring for elderly relatives as well as for children.

The only unhappy family is Scrooge's own. The boy Scrooge is first seen alone, left in school by a father who does not care enough to bring him home even at Christmas. There is a suggestion that his unhappy childhood might be the cause of his closed, harsh nature.

Key Quotations to Learn

What would I not have given to be one of them! (Stave 2)

They were happy, grateful, pleased with one another, and contented with the time. (Stave 3)

An old, old man and woman, with their children and their children's children, and another generation beyond that, all decked out gaily in their holiday attire. (Stave 3)

Summary

- The happy families contrast with Scrooge's isolation.
- Love is shown between married couples.
- Large families are idealised.
- Scrooge's own unhappy childhood has helped to make him what he is.

Sample Analysis

Dickens conveys the happiness of the Cratchits at Christmas in a long sentence that describes their preparations for dinner. He uses **parallel phrasing** to create a sense of breathless excitement. A series of **clauses** separated by semicolons describe what each member of the family does. The **active verbs** such as 'sweetened', 'took' and 'dusted', show their willing involvement and cooperation in creating a meal that is an expression of their love for each other.

Questions

QUICK TEST
1. Which two large families are shown in the novel?
2. Why is the contrast between Scrooge's life and family life more telling at Christmas?
3. How many generations are present at the miner's Christmas?
4. How is Scrooge's father's lack of care for him shown?

EXAM PRACTICE
Using at least one of the 'Key Quotations to Learn', write a paragraph exploring how family life is presented in *A Christmas Carol*.

Death

You must be able to: explore how the theme of death is presented in the novel.

Is the Ghost of Christmas Yet to Come the same as Death?

The description of the Ghost recalls personifications of death as the 'Grim Reaper'.

However, this Ghost has not come to take Scrooge from life but to warn him about how his life will end if he does not change.

How does Dickens present Scrooge's death?

The fact that someone has died is revealed in a conversation between businessmen. Their casual attitude shows that the dead person is not important to them. Then Scrooge is shown a disturbing scene in which a group of people haggle over the dead man's things. Their language and attitude show a lack of respect and even contempt for the dead man. A couple who owe him money are glad he is dead.

Confronted by the man's deathbed, Scrooge is unable to look at the body, delaying the revelation that it is his body. He lies in a dark empty house with no-one to mourn him. Even the graveyard in which he is buried is uncared for.

Scrooge's 'death' can be seen as the symbolic death of the old Scrooge. He has to die in order to be re-born as a better man.

Dickens addresses Death directly, asserting it has no power over the good.

How does Dickens present Tiny Tim's death?

Tiny Tim's death is introduced by a conversation between Mrs Cratchit and her other children. They are concerned about each other, especially Bob, and they remember Tim with affection.

The description of Bob sitting at the dead child's bedside is not 'terrifying' like Scrooge's deathbed. It is peaceful and Bob leaves it feeling 'reconciled'.

The graveyard where Tim is to be buried contrasts with the site of Scrooge's grave. Bob says it would do his wife good to see it.

The Cratchits vow never to forget Tim, and Dickens, addressing him directly, says that his 'essence' comes from God.

How is life after death presented?

The appearance of Marley's ghost suggests that people's behaviour influences what happens to them after death. Although most Christians do not believe in ghosts, this supports the Christian idea of life after death.

Dickens also writes about good deeds living on, showing that those who do good can still have influence after death.

Key Quotations to Learn

He lay in the dark, empty house, with not a man, a woman or a child to say he was kind to me in this or that ... (Stave 4)

Oh, cold, cold, rigid, dreadful Death, set up thine altar here ... (Stave 4)

Spirit of Tiny Tim, thy childish essence was from God! (Stave 4)

Summary

- The deaths of Scrooge and Tiny Tim are contrasted.
- Nobody cares about Scrooge and he dies alone but Tim is remembered and loved.
- People's good deeds live on after them.
- The depiction of Marley's ghost suggests there is an afterlife in which people are rewarded or punished.

Sample Analysis

The 'dark empty house' where Scrooge's body lies is contrasted with Tiny Tim's room, which is 'lighted cheerfully'. The imagery of light and dark conveys the contrasting nature of Scrooge and Tiny Tim. Scrooge lies with 'not a man, not a woman, not a child' to mourn him, whereas, when Bob goes up to see Tim there are 'signs of someone having been there lately'. Bob's kissing of Tim's face clearly demonstrates the 'tenderness' that Scrooge has asked to see.

Questions

QUICK TEST
1. Which two of the following words describe people's reactions to Scrooge's death? Respectful; uncaring; glad; sad.
2. Who is shown mourning Scrooge?
3. How does Bob feel after sitting by Tim's bed?
4. Whose appearance suggests the existence of life after death?

EXAM PRACTICE
Using at least one of the 'Key Quotations to Learn', write a paragraph explaining how reactions to death are presented in A Christmas Carol.

Responsibility

You must be able to: explore how the theme of responsibility is presented in the novel.

What is meant by responsibility?

Being responsible means being accountable for your actions and understanding they have consequences. In *A Christmas Carol*, Scrooge is shown that his actions have consequences for others.

Is it only Scrooge who is responsible?

In some cases, Scrooge is personally responsible for the effects of his behaviour on other people.

In others cases, the responsibility is shared by many including, by implication, the reader.

For what is Scrooge personally responsible?

As his employer, Scrooge is responsible for Bob Cratchit's poor working conditions and low pay. In this, he is a typical nineteenth century employer. Dickens shows the consequences of low pay on Bob's family. We are not told exactly how Scrooge can be responsible for Tiny Tim's plight. We might infer that if Bob could afford better living conditions and medical treatment, Tiny Tim's condition would improve.

In Stave 4, the effect of Scrooge's harshness in business is shown by the misery of Caroline and her husband, who face poverty because they cannot pay him back.

Scrooge is also responsible for his own misery. His greed is the cause of the end of his engagement to Belle, but it is he, and not she, who is left alone. His rejection of Fred's friendship also affects Scrooge himself more than Fred.

In Stave 4, the lack of grief caused by his death and the dislike shown for him after it are the result of his behaviour to others.

For what is Scrooge responsible as a member of society?

The Ghost of Christmas Present states that 'Man' is responsible for the existence of Ignorance and Want. No group or section of society is blamed, implying that everyone has a responsibility to deal with society's problems.

Scrooge's claim that he makes his contribution already by supporting prisons and workhouses, presumably by paying tax, is rejected as not being enough.

Dickens's message is that we have all helped to cause the problems of society and we should all help to solve them.

Key Quotations to Learn

'I help to support the establishments I have mentioned – they cost enough ...' (Scrooge: Stave 1)

'Who suffers by his ill whims? Himself always.' (Fred: Stave 3)

'Men's courses will foreshadow certain ends, to which, if persevered in, they must lead ...' (Scrooge: Stave 4)

Summary

- Scrooge is personally responsible for the Cratchits' problems.
- He is also responsible for his own misery and unpopularity.
- Other characters show a sense of responsibility.
- We are all responsible for society's problems, especially poverty.

Sample Analysis

When Scrooge asks whether the Union workhouses, the **Treadmill** and the Poor Law still operate, he is effectively saying that he personally has no responsibility for others in society. He states that he helps to 'support' them and that they 'cost enough'. As he makes his contribution to the government, he is not interested in discussing the plight of the poor as it is not his 'business'. The portly gentlemen, on the other hand, try to make up for the inadequacy of the Poor Law both by questioning it ('But you might know it') and providing practical help for the poor.

Questions

QUICK TEST
1. How might Scrooge be responsible for Tiny Tim's condition?
2. Who is responsible for the fact that no one cares about Scrooge's death?
3. Which characters show a responsible attitude to society in general?
4. When Dickens writes that 'Man' is responsible, who does he mean?

EXAM PRACTICE
Using at least one of the 'Key Quotations to Learn', write a paragraph explaining how the theme of responsibility is presented in A Christmas Carol.

Redemption

You must be able to: explore how the theme of redemption is presented in the novel.

What is meant by redemption?

Redemption means being saved from sin or evil.

Christians believe that Jesus Christ was sent to earth to redeem us. To be saved people must be sorry for their sins and live good lives.

Why does Scrooge need to be redeemed?

Scrooge is described in Stave 1 as a 'sinner'. His chief sin is avarice, one of the seven deadly sins of Christian tradition. His lack of compassion is also sinful.

If Scrooge is not saved, he will end up like Marley, who is being punished after his death.

How is Scrooge redeemed?

There are three stages in Scrooge's redemption, represented by the three Ghosts.

First, Scrooge must confront his past, understand where he has gone wrong and atone for his actions. Seeing Fan makes Scrooge think of her son, Fred, and how he treats him. Seeing Mr Fezziwig makes Scrooge think of how he treats Bob Cratchit. Reliving the scene with Belle shows Scrooge just how sinful his desire for money is.

The Ghost of Christmas Present makes Scrooge realise that he can change his way of life but also makes him confront the results of his actions.

The Ghost of Christmas Yet to Come shows him what will happen if he does not reform, making him determined to change.

Tiny Tim is especially important in Scrooge's redemption. As an innocent child, Tim is linked to Christ, whose birth on Christmas day is celebrated because it led to the redemption of mankind.

Who redeems Scrooge?

The Ghosts can be seen as messengers from God. The Ghost of Christmas Past says his business is Scrooge's 'reclamation'. Dickens states that Tiny Tim's 'childish essence' is from God.

However, Scrooge can only be saved by his own actions. He learns lessons from the Ghosts and changes his behaviour, putting right some of the wrongs he has committed in the past.

The fact that the visions shown in Stave 4 do not come about shows that Scrooge is forgiven for his past sins and has been redeemed.

Key Quotations to Learn

'Your reclamation ...' (The Ghost of Christmas Past: Stave 2)

'I should like to be able to say a word or two to my clerk just now.' (Scrooge: Stave 2)

'I am not the man I was.' (Scrooge: Stave 4)

Summary

- Scrooge is a sinner and needs to be redeemed.
- The Ghosts are sent to save him.
- Tiny Tim, as an innocent child, has a special role in Scrooge's redemption.
- Scrooge can only be saved if he changes his way of life.

Sample Analysis

At the end of Stave 4, Scrooge asks the Ghost a series of questions. At first, the Ghost is 'immovable'. However, when Scrooge begs to know whether he is past all hope, its hand shakes, suggesting that perhaps things are not certain. After Scrooge asks whether he might change the 'shadows' by living 'an altered life', the hand trembles. It is now described as 'kind', **implying** that the Ghost has been sent to help Scrooge. Nevertheless, the reader is left uncertain about whether Scrooge has managed to redeem himself with the help of the Ghosts.

Questions

QUICK TEST
1. Which deadly sin is Scrooge guilty of?
2. What is Tiny Tim's significance in Scrooge's redemption?
3. How do we know that Scrooge has been redeemed?

EXAM PRACTICE
Using at least one of the 'Key Quotations to Learn', write a paragraph explaining how the theme of redemption is presented in *A Christmas Carol*.

Tips and Assessment Objectives

You must be able to: understand how to approach the exam question and meet the requirements of the mark scheme.

Quick tips

- You will be given one question on *A Christmas Carol*. There will be a short extract from the novel, followed by the question.

- The question will probably focus on a character or theme. Whatever its focus, you will be expected to show that you understand the novel's characters, themes and context.

- The question will have two bullet points. One of these will ask you to write about the extract and the other will ask you to write about the novel as a whole.

- Make sure you know what the question is asking you. Underline key words.

- You should spend about 50 minutes on your response. Allow yourself five minutes to plan your answer so there is some structure to your essay.

- All your paragraphs should contain a clear idea, a relevant reference to the novel (ideally a quotation) and analysis of how Dickens conveys this idea. Whenever possible, you should link your comments to the novel's context.

- It can sometimes help, after each paragraph, to quickly re-read the question to keep yourself focused on the exam task.

- Keep your writing concise. If you waste time 'waffling' you will not be able to include the full range of analysis and understanding that the mark scheme requires.

- It is a good idea to remember what the mark scheme is asking of you.

AO1: Understand and respond to the novel (12 marks)

This is all about coming up with a range of points that match the question, supporting your ideas with references from the novel and writing your essay in a mature, academic style.

Lower	Middle	Upper
The essay has some good ideas that are mostly relevant. Some quotations and references are used to support the ideas.	A clear essay that always focuses on the exam question. Quotations and references support ideas effectively. The response refers to different points in the novel.	A convincing, well-structured essay that answers the question fully. Quotations and references are well-chosen and integrated into sentences. The response covers the whole novel.

AO2: Analyse effects of Dickens's language, form and structure (12 marks)

You need to comment on how Dickens uses specific words, language techniques, sentence structures and the narrative structure to get his ideas across to the reader.

Lower	Middle	Upper
Identification of some different methods used by Dickens to convey meaning. Some subject terminology.	Explanation of Dickens's different methods. Clear understanding of the effects of these methods. Accurate use of subject terminology.	Analysis of the full range of Dickens's methods. Thorough exploration of the effects of these methods. Accurate range of subject terminology.

AO3: Understand the relationship between the novel and its contexts (6 marks)

For this part of the mark scheme, you need to show your understanding of how the characters' and Dickens's ideas and attitudes relate to the time when he was writing (1843).

Lower	Middle	Upper
Some awareness of how ideas in the novel link to its context.	References to relevant aspects of context show a clear understanding.	Exploration is linked to specific aspects of the novel's contexts to show a detailed understanding.

1. Answer both parts of the question.

Read this extract from Stave 3 and answer the question that follows. Scrooge and the Ghost of Christmas Present are watching Fred's Christmas party.

'Ha, ha!' laughed Scrooge's nephew. 'Ha, ha, ha!'

If you should happen, by any unlikely chance, to know a man more blest in a laugh than Scrooge's nephew, all I can say is, I should like to know him too. Introduce him to me, and I'll cultivate his acquaintance.

It is a fair, even-handed, noble adjustment of things, that while there is infection in disease and sorrow, there is nothing in the world so irresistibly contagious as laughter and good-humour. When Scrooge's nephew laughed in this way: holding his sides, rolling his head, and twisting his face into the most extravagant contortions: Scrooge's niece, by marriage, laughed as heartily as he. And their assembled friends being not a bit behindhand, roared out lustily.

'Ha, ha! Ha, ha, ha, ha!'

'He said that Christmas was a humbug, as I live!' cried Scrooge's nephew. 'He believed it too!'

'More shame for him, Fred!' said Scrooge's niece, indignantly. Bless those women; they never do anything by halves. They are always in earnest. [...]

'He's a comical old fellow,' said Scrooge's nephew, 'that's the truth: and not so pleasant as he might be. However, his offences carry their own punishment, and I have nothing to say against him.'

'I'm sure he is very rich, Fred,' hinted Scrooge's niece. 'At least you always tell me so.'

'What of that, my dear!' said Scrooge's nephew. 'His wealth is of no use to him. He don't do any good with it. He don't make himself comfortable with it. He hasn't the satisfaction of thinking – ha, ha, ha! – that he is ever going to benefit Us with it.'

'I have no patience with him,' observed Scrooge's niece. Scrooge's niece's sisters, and all the other ladies, expressed the same opinion.

'Oh, I have!' said Scrooge's nephew. 'I am sorry for him; I couldn't be angry with him if I tried. Who suffers by his ill whims? Himself, always. Here, he takes it into his head to dislike us, and he won't come and dine with us. What's the consequence? He don't lose much of a dinner.'

Starting with this extract, explore how Dickens presents Fred as a contrast to Scrooge. Write about:

*   how he presents Fred in this extract
*   how he presents Fred in the novel as a whole.

2. Answer both parts of the question.

Read this extract from Stave 2 and answer the question that follows. Scrooge and the Ghost of Christmas Past watch as Belle releases Scrooge from their engagement.

> *This was not addressed to Scrooge, or to any one whom he could see, but it produced an immediate effect. For again Scrooge saw himself. He was older now; a man in the prime of life. His face had not the harsh and rigid lines of later years; but it had begun to wear the signs of care and avarice. There was an eager, greedy, restless motion in the eye, which showed the passion that had taken root, and where the shadow of the growing tree would fall.*
>
> *He was not alone, but sat by the side of a fair young girl in a mourning-dress: in whose eyes there were tears, which sparkled in the light that shone out of the Ghost of Christmas Past.*
>
> *'It matters little,' she said, softly. 'To you, very little. Another idol has displaced me; and if it can cheer and comfort you in time to come, as I would have tried to do, I have no just cause to grieve.'*
>
> *'What Idol has displaced you?' he rejoined.*
>
> *'A golden one.'*
>
> *'This is the even-handed dealing of the world!' he said. 'There is nothing on which it is so hard as poverty; and there is nothing it professes to condemn with such severity as the pursuit of wealth!'*
>
> *'You fear the world too much,' she answered, gently. 'All your other hopes have merged into the hope of being beyond the chance of its sordid reproach. I have seen your nobler aspirations fall off one by one, until the master-passion, Gain, engrosses you. Have I not?'*
>
> *'What then?' he retorted. 'Even if I have grown so much wiser, what then? I am not changed towards you.'*
>
> *She shook her head.*
>
> *'Am I?'*
>
> *'Our contract is an old one. It was made when we were both poor and content to be so, until, in good season, we could improve our worldly fortune by our patient industry. You are changed. When it was made, you were another man.'*
>
> *'I was a boy,' he said impatiently.*

Starting with this extract, explain how Dickens writes about how Scrooge changes from boyhood up to the death of Marley. Write about:
- how he presents Scrooge in this extract
- how he presents Scrooge in the novel as a whole.

3. Answer both parts of the question.

Read this extract from Stave 3 and answer the question that follows. Here, the Ghost of Christmas Present shows Scrooge how different groups of people celebrate Christmas.

'What place is this?' asked Scrooge.

'A place where Miners live, who labour in the bowels of the earth,' returned the Spirit. 'But they know me. See!'

A light shone from the window of a hut, and swiftly they advanced towards it. Passing through the wall of mud and stone, they found a cheerful company assembled round a glowing fire. An old, old man and woman, with their children and their children's children, and another generation beyond that, all decked out gaily in their holiday attire. The old man, in a voice that seldom rose above the howling of the wind upon the barren waste, was singing them a Christmas song: it had been a very old song when he was a boy; and from time to time they all joined in the chorus. So surely as they raised their voices, the old man got quite blithe and loud; and so surely as they stopped, his vigour sank again.

The Spirit did not tarry here, but bade Scrooge hold his robe, and passing on above the moor, sped whither? Not to sea? To sea. To Scrooge's horror, looking back, he saw the last of the land, a frightful range of rocks, behind them; and his ears were deafened by the thundering of water, as it rolled, and roared, and raged among the dreadful caverns it had worn, and fiercely tried to undermine the earth.

Built upon a dismal reef of sunken rocks, some league or so from shore, on which the waters chafed and dashed, the wild year through, there stood a solitary lighthouse. Great heaps of sea-weed clung to its base, and storm-birds – born of the wind one might suppose, as sea-weed of the water – rose and fell about it, like the waves they skimmed.

But even here, two men who watched the light had made a fire, that through the loophole in the thick stone wall shed out a ray of brightness on the awful sea. Joining their horny hands over the rough table at which they sat, they wished each other Merry Christmas in their can of grog; and one of them: the elder, too, with his face all damaged and scarred with hard weather, as the figure-head of an old ship might be: struck up a sturdy song that was like a Gale in itself.

Starting with this extract, explain what is meant by the spirit of Christmas and how Dickens writes about it. Write about:

* how he writes about the spirit of Christmas in the extract
* how he writes about the spirit of Christmas in the novel as a whole.

4. Answer both parts of the question.

Read this extract from Stave 4 and answer the question that follows. Here, the Cratchits are mourning the death of Tiny Tim.

> *They drew about the fire, and talked; the girls and mother working still. Bob told them of the extraordinary kindness of Mr Scrooge's nephew, whom he had scarcely seen but once, and who, meeting him in the street that day, and seeing that he looked a little – 'just a little down you know,' said Bob, inquired what had happened to distress him. 'On which,' said Bob, 'for he is the pleasantest-spoken gentleman you ever heard, I told him. "I am heartily sorry for it, Mr Cratchit," he said, "and heartily sorry for your good wife." By the bye, how he ever knew that, I don't know.'*
>
> *'Knew what, my dear?'*
>
> *'Why, that you were a good wife,' replied Bob.*
>
> *'Everybody knows that.' said Peter.*
>
> *'Very well observed, my boy!' cried Bob. 'I hope they do. "Heartily sorry," he said, "for your good wife. If I can be of service to you in any way," he said, giving me his card, "that's where I live. Pray come to me." 'Now, it wasn't,' cried Bob, 'for the sake of anything he might be able to do for us, so much as for his kind way, that this was quite delightful. It really seemed as if he had known our Tiny Tim, and felt with us.'*
>
> *'I'm sure he's a good soul!' said Mrs Cratchit.*
>
> *'You would be surer of it, my dear,' returned Bob, 'if you saw and spoke to him. I shouldn't be at all surprised, mark what I say, if he got Peter a better situation.'*
>
> *'Only hear that, Peter,' said Mrs Cratchit.*
>
> *'And then,' cried one of the girls, 'Peter will be keeping company with some one, and setting up for himself.'*
>
> *'Get along with you!' retorted Peter, grinning.*
>
> *'It's just as likely as not,' said Bob, 'one of these days; though there's plenty of time for that, my dear. But however and whenever we part from one another, I am sure we shall none of us forget poor Tiny Tim – shall we – or this first parting that there was among us?'*
>
> *'Never, father!' cried they all.*
>
> *'And I know,' said Bob, 'I know, my dears, that when we recollect how patient and how mild he was; although he was a little, little child; we shall not quarrel easily among ourselves, and forget poor Tiny Tim in doing it.'*
>
> *'No, never, father!' they all cried again.*
>
> *'I am very happy' said little Bob, 'I am very happy!'*
>
> *Mrs Cratchit kissed him, his daughters kissed him, the two young Cratchits kissed him, and Peter and himself shook hands. Spirit of Tiny Tim, thy childish essence was from God!*

Starting with this extract, how far do you think that Dickens presents the Cratchits as the ideal family? Write about:

- how he presents the Cratchit family in this extract
- how he presents the Cratchit family in the novel as a whole.

5. Answer both parts of the question.

Read this extract from Stave 2 and answer the question that follows. Here, the Ghost of Christmas Past has taken Scrooge to see himself as a boy.

'The school is not quite deserted,' said the Ghost. 'A solitary child, neglected by his friends, is left there still.'

Scrooge said he knew it. And he sobbed.

They left the high-road, by a well-remembered lane, and soon approached a mansion of dull red brick, with a little weathercock-surmounted cupola, on the roof, and a bell hanging in it. It was a large house, but one of broken fortunes; for the spacious offices were little used, their walls were damp and mossy, their windows broken, and their gates decayed. Fowls clucked and strutted in the stables; and the coach-houses and sheds were over-run with grass. Nor was it more retentive of its ancient state, within; for entering the dreary hall, and glancing through the open doors of many rooms, they found them poorly furnished, cold, and vast. There was an earthy savour in the air, a chilly bareness in the place, which associated itself somehow with too much getting up by candle-light, and not too much to eat.

They went, the Ghost and Scrooge, across the hall, to a door at the back of the house. It opened before them, and disclosed a long, bare, melancholy room, made barer still by lines of plain deal forms and desks. At one of these a lonely boy was reading near a feeble fire; and Scrooge sat down upon a form, and wept to see his poor forgotten self as he used to be.

Not a latent echo in the house, not a squeak and scuffle from the mice behind the panelling, not a drip from the half-thawed water-spout in the dull yard behind, not a sigh among the leafless boughs of one despondent poplar, not the idle swinging of an empty store-house door, no, not a clicking in the fire, but fell upon the heart of Scrooge with a softening influence, and gave a freer passage to his tears.

Starting with this extract, to what extent do you think that Dickens presents Scrooge as a sympathetic character? Write about:

* how he presents Scrooge in this extract
* how he presents Scrooge in the novel as a whole.

6. Read this extract from Stave 1 and answer the question that follows. Here, Scrooge is visited by two gentlemen who are collecting for the poor.

'At this festive season of the year, Mr Scrooge,' said the gentleman, taking up a pen, 'it is more than usually desirable that we should make some slight provision for the Poor and destitute, who suffer greatly at the present time. Many thousands are in want of common necessaries; hundreds of thousands are in want of common comforts, sir.'

'Are there no prisons?' asked Scrooge.

'Plenty of prisons,' said the gentleman, laying down the pen again.

'And the Union workhouses?' demanded Scrooge. 'Are they still in operation?'

'They are. Still,' returned the gentleman, 'I wish I could say they were not.'

'The Treadmill and the Poor Law are in full vigour, then?' said Scrooge.

'Both very busy, sir.'

'Oh! I was afraid, from what you said at first, that something had occurred to stop them in their useful course,' said Scrooge. 'I'm very glad to hear it.'

'Under the impression that they scarcely furnish Christian cheer of mind or body to the multitude,' returned the gentleman, 'a few of us are endeavouring to raise a fund to buy the Poor some meat and drink, and means of warmth. We choose this time, because it is a time, of all others, when Want is keenly felt, and Abundance rejoices. What shall I put you down for?'

'Nothing!' Scrooge replied.

'You wish to be anonymous?'

'I wish to be left alone,' said Scrooge. 'Since you ask me what I wish, gentlemen, that is my answer. I don't make merry myself at Christmas and I can't afford to make idle people merry. I help to support the establishments I have mentioned: they cost enough: and those who are badly off must go there.'

'Many can't go there; and many would rather die.'

'If they would rather die,' said Scrooge, 'they had better do it, and decrease the surplus population. Besides – excuse me – I don't know that.'

'But you might know it,' observed the gentleman.

'It's not my business,' Scrooge returned. 'It's enough for a man to understand his own business, and not to interfere with other people's. Mine occupies me constantly. Good afternoon, gentlemen!'

Starting with this extract, explore how Dickens writes about the theme of responsibility. Write about:
- how he writes about responsibility in this extract
- how he writes about responsibility in the novel as a whole.

Planning a Character Question Response

You must be able to: understand what an exam question is asking you and prepare your response.

How might an exam question on character be phrased?

Question 1 (page 56) and Question 5 (page 60) are typical character questions, focusing on a single character. Question 4 focuses on a group of characters and refers to an important theme in the novel. Remember that the themes and characters are not mutually exclusive. A character question will require some discussion of themes; a theme question will require discussion of character.

Look again at Question 5.

Starting with this extract, to what extent do you think that Dickens presents Scrooge as a sympathetic character? Write about:

*   how he presents Scrooge in this extract
*   how he presents Scrooge in the novel as a whole.   [30 marks]

How do I work out what to do?

The focus of this question is clear: Scrooge and the extent to which he is sympathetic.

The bullet points make it clear that your answer should be equally divided between analysis of the extract and of the novel as a whole.

For AO1, you need to display a clear understanding of what Scrooge is like, to what extent the reader sympathises with him in the extract and to what extent he is sympathetic in the rest of the novel.

For AO2, you need to analyse the different ways in which Dickens's use of language, structure and form show what Scrooge is like and establish sympathy for him. You should include short quotations from the extract and, ideally, a few from elsewhere in the novel.

Remember to link your comments to the novel's context to achieve your AO3 marks.

How can I plan my essay?

You have approximately 50 minutes to write your essay.

You should spend the first few minutes reading the extracts and underlining or highlighting words or phrases that you want to analyse. Then you might want to spend a few minutes (no more than five) writing a quick plan. You could number the points before you start and use them in that order and/or you could tick them off as you cover each one.

You can plan in whatever way you find most useful. Spider diagrams are particularly popular; look at the examples opposite.

Scrooge as a sympathetic character

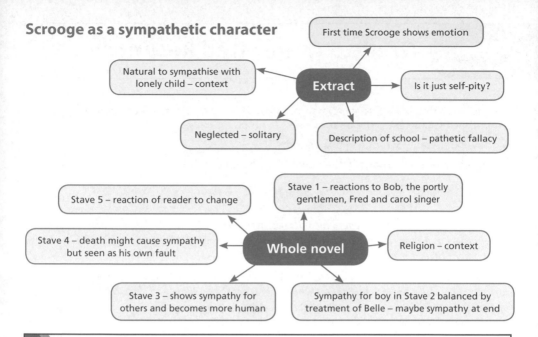

Extract
- First time Scrooge shows emotion
- Is it just self-pity?
- Description of school – pathetic fallacy
- Neglected – solitary
- Natural to sympathise with lonely child – context

Whole novel
- Stave 1 – reactions to Bob, the portly gentlemen, Fred and carol singer
- Religion – context
- Sympathy for boy in Stave 2 balanced by treatment of Belle – maybe sympathy at end
- Stave 3 – shows sympathy for others and becomes more human
- Stave 4 – death might cause sympathy but seen as his own fault
- Stave 5 – reaction of reader to change

Summary

- Make sure you know what the focus of the essay is.
- Remember to analyse how ideas are conveyed by Dickens.
- Try to relate your ideas to the novel's social and historical context.

Questions

QUICK TEST
1. What key skills do you need to show in your answer?
2. What are the benefits of quickly planning your essay?
3. Why is it better to have learned quotations for the exam?

EXAM PRACTICE
Plan a response to question 1 (page 56).
Starting with this extract, explore how Dickens presents Fred as a contrast to Scrooge.
Write about:
- how he presents Fred in this extract
- how he presents Fred in the novel as a whole. [30 marks]

Grade 5 Annotated Response

Starting with this extract, to what extent do you think that Dickens presents Scrooge as a sympathetic character? Write about:

- how he presents Scrooge in this extract
- how he presents Scrooge in the novel as a whole.

[30 marks]

Scrooge shows emotion at the beginning of the extract; 'he sobbed'. This is the first time the reader sees that he has feelings apart from anger. However, he is crying at the thought of his own loneliness so you might think it is just self-pity (1).

The way that Dickens describes the school increases the sense of Scrooge's sad childhood. He uses adjectives like 'dull', 'broken' and 'damp', which show that the building is neglected just like Scrooge was neglected (2). He emphasises how cold it is and gives a picture of a very uncomfortable life. The reader would feel sorry for a child who had to live like this (3).

Dickens uses the word 'melancholy', which means sad, to describe the room. It also describes Scrooge and when he sees himself he 'wept to see his poor forgotten self'. The repetition in the last paragraph of 'not a' builds up a depressing picture and it has a 'softening influence' on Scrooge and makes him weep (4). The reader would probably also become sympathetic to him now as they understand what sort of childhood he had (5).

This is a big change in how we see Scrooge. In the first Stave, he is described in a very unsympathetic way (6). His appearance is unattractive and like his nature, 'a grasping old sinner'. He treats everyone badly. He doesn't let Bob have enough coal, he turns down Fred's kindness and he will not give money to the poor. Also, he does not like Christmas, calling it 'humbug'. This would have been shocking at the time. He is also made fun of (7). When he sees Marley's ghost and hears his warning about the future he is still not very sympathetic.

After this extract he sees himself with Fezziwig. This might help him become sympathetic because he is shown as human, having fun and enjoying Christmas. However, when we see him with Belle we might lose sympathy again as he is now shown as loving money more than her. She behaves better than him although she has more to lose, being a woman without wealth. At the end of the chapter, though, there might be sympathy for him when he sees how happy Belle is and gets very upset (8).

In the rest of the novel, he gets more sympathetic as a character. In Stave 3 he starts to show sympathy for other people, like Tiny Tim. He regrets things he has done and said, learning from the Ghosts. In Stave 4 he sees his own lonely death. It would be hard not to have sympathy for him as Dickens describes the dark lonely room with no mourners and how little everyone thinks of him, but the reader might still be thinking that it's all his own fault (9).

In the end, although he starts as a very unsympathetic character, I think Dickens gradually makes him more sympathetic by showing how he became what he is and by showing his human side and that he can change (10).

1. The first paragraph has a clear idea and is supported by a reference to the extract. AO1

2. Clear explanation of the writer's use of language, using appropriate terminology ('adjectives') and references. AO2/AO1

3. Clear response to question (focus on sympathy). AO1

4. Good explanation of the writer's use of language, using appropriate terminology (repetition). AO1/AO2

5. Clear focus on question again. AO1

6. Reference to narrative structure. AO2

7. Good attempt at using a range of quotations not taken from extract. Sustained response to question. A brief reference to context, not developed. AO1/AO3

8. Response to question sustained in this paragraph. Candidate shows awareness of how sympathy can change. No quotations but appropriate references to text. Another reference to context. AO1/AO2

9. This paragraph continues to develop ideas about sympathy and how readers might react. There is an awareness of narrative structure but no analysis of language techniques. AO1/AO2

10. A clear concluding paragraph, showing understanding of the novel's narrative structure. AO1/AO2

> ## Questions
>
> EXAM PRACTICE
> Choose a paragraph of this essay. Read it through a few times then try to rewrite and improve it. You might:
> * Improve the sophistication of the language, for example by using more varied vocabulary, and the clarity of expression.
> * Replace a reference with a quotation or use a better quotation.
> * Ensure quotations are embedded in the sentence.
> * Provide more detailed, or a wider range of, analysis.
> * Use more subject terminology.
> * Link context to the analysis more effectively.

Grade 7+ Annotated Response

A proportion of the best top-band answers will be awarded Grade 8 or Grade 9. To achieve this, you should aim for a sophisticated, fluid and nuanced response that displays flair and originality.

Starting with this extract, to what extent do you think that Dickens presents Scrooge as a sympathetic character? Write about:

- how he presents Scrooge in this extract
- how he presents Scrooge in the novel as a whole.   [30 marks]

In this extract, Dickens uses pathetic fallacy to give a sense of Scrooge's sad childhood. Adjectives like 'dull', 'broken' and 'damp', showing how the building is neglected, also convey the neglect of the child by his father. The literal imagery, emphasising cold and discomfort, creates sympathy for a child who has to live like this (1).

*Dickens describes the school room as 'melancholy', a word he also uses as a **transferred epithet** in Stave 1, when he describes the adult Scrooge's 'melancholy dinner'. In Stave 1, there is a feeling that he has chosen to be miserable, whereas here, as a child, he has not (2). Concern about the treatment of children in Victorian times is a recurring theme of the novel and here Dickens shows that not only poor children suffer. Middle-class attitudes to children can also lead to neglect and suffering (3).*

*In the last paragraph, the use of **anaphora**, each phrase beginning with 'not a', emphasises negativity and builds up a depressing picture (4). The scene's 'softening influence' on Scrooge could have a similar effect on readers, although the fact that Scrooge is weeping about 'his poor forgotten self' reminds us that his sympathy is for himself, not others. Nevertheless, readers might empathise with him because we see that he is capable of emotion and because we now have an understanding of his childhood and its influence on his character (5).*

This is a turning point in how we see Scrooge. At the start of the novel, he is an extremely unsympathetic character (6). The description of his physical appearance, reflecting his nature, is repulsive as well as comic: 'The cold within him froze his old features'. His actions in the first stave confirm that he is a 'covetous old sinner' as we are shown his reactions to his clerk, his nephew, the men collecting for charity and a carol singer. He alienates everybody to the extent that even the beggars' dogs avoid him (7). His attitude to Christmas ('Humbug!') would further alienate Dickens's readers, perhaps more when the novel was written than now, as the religious aspect of the feast would matter to more people (8).

After this extract, readers' sympathies might waver. Seeing Scrooge enjoying Christmas with the Fezziwigs helps him become sympathetic because he is shown as human. However, when we see him with Belle we might lose sympathy again as he has now made money his 'idol'. At this point, sympathy is with Belle, who acts honourably and risks her own future. At the end of the chapter, though, many readers' sympathy might swing back towards Scrooge as he becomes upset at seeing Belle's happiness and realises how much happier he could be (9).

In the rest of the novel, he continues to gain sympathy as he himself shows sympathy to others. In Stave 3, he is again moved by the plight of a child, but this time he feels not for himself but for Tiny Tim (10). He regrets things he has done and said and, as he develops a sense of responsibility, it is easier to empathise with his plight. In Stave 4, the description of the 'dark empty house' where his body lies 'unwatched, unwept, uncared for' is shocking and horrific (11). Although there may still be an element in readers' reactions of thinking that he deserves what he gets, it would be difficult not to be moved by his anguished reaction and determination to change (12).

1. A clear, strong point focused on the question. Uses subject terminology accurately. Appropriate use of quotations. AO1/AO2

2. Sophisticated subject terminology used accurately. Relates a point to another part of the novel. AO1/AO2

3. Scrooge's situation is related to the novel's context. AO3

4. Most sophisticated subject terminology used to analyse the effect of the writing. AO2

5. Thoughtful and focused consideration of what sympathy means. AO1

6. Consideration of the novel's narrative structure. AO2

7. The candidate is now moving to the second part of the question and is considering the question in the light of the novel as a whole. AO1

8. Ideas linked to specific aspect of context. AO3

9. A thoughtful exploration of another part of the novel and the effect of the novel's narrative structure. AO1/AO2/AO3

10. Refers to a point made earlier in the answer, keeping focused on the question. AO1

11. Another part of the novel explored, using embedded quotations. AO1/AO2

12. The final sentence acknowledges that there may be different interpretations and reaches a balanced conclusion about the extent to which the character is sympathetic. AO1

Questions

EXAM PRACTICE

Spend about 50 minutes writing an answer to question 1 (page 56).
Starting with this extract, explore how Dickens presents Fred as a contrast to Scrooge. Write about:
- how he presents Fred in this extract
- how he presents Fred in the novel as a whole.   [30 marks]

Remember to use the plan you have already prepared.

Planning a Theme Question Response

You must be able to: understand what an exam question is asking you and prepare your response.

How might an exam question on theme be phrased?

Questions 2, 3 and 6 are typical of theme-based exam questions. Question 4, about the Cratchit family, is focused equally on character and theme. But remember that any question on *A Christmas Carol* will almost always involve a discussion of character. Look again at question 6 on page 61.

Starting with this extract, explore how Dickens writes about the theme of responsibility. Write about:

- how he writes about responsibility in this extract
- how he writes about responsibility in the novel as a whole. [30 marks]

How do I work out what to do?

The focus of this question is responsibility.

The bullet points remind you to write about the extract from the novel, which requires close analysis, and the rest of the novel.

The word 'how' focuses you on the writer's methods.

For AO1, you need to demonstrate a clear understanding of what is meant by responsibility and the attitudes of the characters, especially Scrooge, towards it.

For AO2, 'how' makes it clear that you need to analyse the different ways in which Dickens uses language, structure and form to explore ideas about responsibility. You must include short quotations from the extract. Ideally, you should also include some quotations from other parts of the novel but, if necessary, you can make a clear reference to a specific part of the novel.

You also need to remember to link your comments to the novel's context to achieve your AO3 marks.

How can I plan my essay?

You have approximately 50 minutes to write your essay.

This is not long but you should spend the first five minutes or so reading the extract and writing a quick plan. This will help you to focus your thoughts and produce a well-structured essay

You can plan in whatever way you find most useful. Some students like to just make a quick list of points and then re-number them into a logical order. Spider diagrams are particularly popular; look at the example opposite.

Responsibility

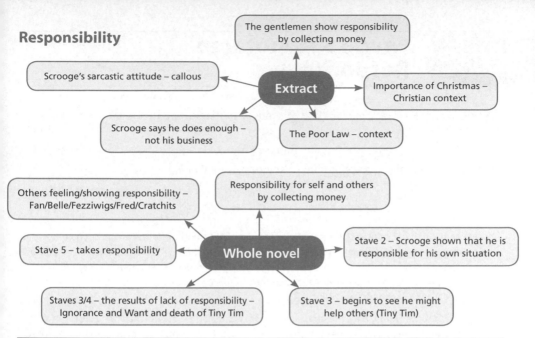

The gentlemen show responsibility by collecting money

Scrooge's sarcastic attitude – callous

Extract

Importance of Christmas – Christian context

Scrooge says he does enough – not his business

The Poor Law – context

Others feeling/showing responsibility – Fan/Belle/Fezziwigs/Fred/Cratchits

Responsibility for self and others by collecting money

Stave 5 – takes responsibility

Whole novel

Stave 2 – Scrooge shown that he is responsible for his own situation

Staves 3/4 – the results of lack of responsibility – Ignorance and Want and death of Tiny Tim

Stave 3 – begins to see he might help others (Tiny Tim)

Summary

- Make sure you know what the focus of the essay is.
- Remember to analyse how Dickens conveys ideas.
- Try to relate your ideas to the novel's social and historical context.

Questions

QUICK TEST
1. What key skills do you need to show in your answer?
2. What are the benefits of quickly planning your essay?
3. Why is it better to have learned quotations for the exam?

EXAM PRACTICE
Plan a response to question 3 (page 58).
Starting with this extract, explain what is meant by the spirit of Christmas and how Dickens writes about it. Write about:
- how he writes about the spirit of Christmas in the extract
- how he writes about the spirit of Christmas in the novel as a whole. [30 marks]

Starting with this extract, explore how Dickens writes about the theme of responsibility. Write about:

- how he writes about responsibility in this extract
- how he writes about responsibility in the novel as a whole.

[30 marks]

The two gentlemen are collecting for charity. This shows that they have a sense of responsibility because they care about 'the poor and destitute' (1). The gentleman with the pen explains to Scrooge why poor people need help at Christmas because they need 'common necessaries'. He says it is especially important to help others at Christmas. This links to the idea that Christmas is about giving and Christians should help others (2).

Scrooge, on the other hand, does not show a sense of responsibility. He asks a lot of questions about prisons and workhouses. He is very sarcastic when he says 'I was afraid from what you said at first that something had occurred to stop them' (3). However, the gentlemen do not catch on to this and just answer the question by saying the poor people need more 'Christian cheer'. Dickens was very angry about the Poor Law, which had just come in when he wrote the book, because it made things harder than they had been for poor people (4).

Scrooge does not agree with this. He thinks it is enough that the government provides prisons and workhouses. When the gentleman tells him people would rather die than go to the workhouse he says 'they had better do it'. This shocks the reader. He then adds that he does not know if what the gentlemen say is true, which shows that he has no interest in others. What happens to others is 'not his business', showing that he does not feel responsible for what happens in society (5).

The Ghosts teach him how to be responsible. The Ghost of Christmas Past shows him how other people take a more responsible attitude. Fan shows responsibility to her family by collecting Scrooge from school. Mr Fezziwig is an example of a responsible employer who looks after his workers. Belle shows more responsibility than Scrooge when she breaks off the engagement. She is responsible for her own happiness and he is responsible for how his life turns out (6).

The Ghost of Christmas Present teaches Scrooge about responsibility in two ways. He shows him how poorer people like the Cratchits live. When he sees how ill Tiny Tim is, he starts to think about how he could help others (7). At the end of the stave, the Ghost shocks Scrooge by showing him Ignorance and Want. These are two children who personify the problems of society. He says that they are 'Man's' children, meaning we are responsible for creating these problems and he warns Scrooge that something has to be done about them (8). The Ghost of Christmas Yet to Come shows Scrooge what will happen if he does not show responsibility. Tiny Tim will die and Scrooge himself will die a lonely death (9).

Finally, in the last stave, Scrooge becomes responsible. He changes his own life and he starts to help other people. Dickens shows how much better it is to be part of the world and have a responsible attitude (10).

1. A clear, if simple, point about how the extract relates to the idea of responsibility. AO1
2. Develops the idea of responsibility and relates it to social and historical context. AO1/ AO3
3. Explanation of the writer's use of language, using basic terminology ('questions') and some interpretation. The quotation is a little long but the candidate has now used a range of references. AO1/ AO2
4. Context linked to the explanation. AO3
5. Clear explanation, starting to develop ideas of what responsibility is. Uses quotations effectively. AO1
6. A range of references to another part of the text. Focus on the question is sustained but the candidate could explain more clearly how these examples are linked to the ideas of responsibility discussed earlier. AO1
7. Focuses on the question, showing awareness of the novel's structure. AO1/AO2
8. Sustained focus on question. Explanation of the writer's methods, using appropriate terminology ('personify') and referring closely to another part of the text. Understanding of context implied. AO1/AO2/AO3
9. A brief, undeveloped reference to another part of the text. Focus on question maintained. AO1
10. A neat, if undeveloped, summary. The answer has been clear, consistent and sustained as required at this level. AO1

 Questions

EXAM PRACTICE
Choose a paragraph of this essay. Read it through a few times, then try to rewrite and improve it. You might:
- Improve the sophistication of the language or the clarity of expression.
- Replace a reference with a quotation or use a better quotation.
- Ensure quotations are embedded in the sentence.
- Provide more detailed, or a wider range of, analysis.
- Use more subject terminology.
- Link context to the analysis more effectively.

Grade 7+ Annotated Response

A proportion of the best top-band answers will be awarded Grade 8 or Grade 9. To achieve this, you should aim for a sophisticated, fluid and nuanced response that displays flair and originality.

Starting with this extract, explore how Dickens writes about the theme of responsibility. Write about:

- how he writes about responsibility in this extract
- how he writes about responsibility in the novel as a whole.

[30 marks]

This conversation between Scrooge and the two 'portly gentlemen' demonstrates the conflict between those who feel some responsibility for problems such as poverty and those who do not believe that the welfare of others is their 'business' (1). The gentlemen show responsibility by collecting for the 'poor and destitute'. They seek to make their appeal more effective by mentioning the 'festive season', referring to the traditional (and still current) idea that Christmas is about giving (2).

*Scrooge interrogates the gentlemen with a series of questions, his impolite tone indicated by the verb 'demanded'. His questions about provisions for the poor demonstrate his heartlessness, as the things he mentions – prisons, the treadmill, union workhouses – are examples of how inadequate and cruel the response to poverty had become since the 1834 Poor Law (3). The gentleman answers his sarcasm ('I'm very glad to hear it') with the gentler irony of **litotes**, politely suggesting that these institutions 'scarcely furnish Christian cheer'. Unaware of Scrooge's attitude to Christmas (unlike the reader), he refers to the Christian tradition of taking responsibility for others by offering practical help (4).*

Scrooge claims to 'support' the poor through the 'establishments I have mentioned', a reference to them being maintained by taxes. This argument might seem reasonable but the gentleman argues emotively that 'many would rather die' than go to the workhouse. Scrooge's assertion that it would be better for them to die and 'decrease the surplus population' reflects the idea, common at the time, that poverty was caused by overpopulation and could only be cured by reducing the population. By having Scrooge express it in such a crude and personal manner ('they had better do it') Dickens exposes its callousness. He also questions the truth of what the gentleman has said and says it is not his 'business' to know about it, thereby denying that he has any responsibility for causing the problem of poverty or has any obligation to deal with it (5).

Over the next three staves, the Ghosts teach him how to accept responsibility for his own actions and show a responsible attitude to others. The Ghost of Christmas Past shows him others taking a more responsible attitude, from Fan implying that her father has started to take a more responsible attitude to his children to Mr Fezziwig giving an example of a responsible employer, in contrast with the Scrooge of Stave 1. At the end of the stave, we see two people taking responsibility for their own future when Belle releases Scrooge from their engagement. While she takes the honourable course, and is rewarded with a happy family life, his choice of 'Gain' over love leads to misery and loneliness, a message reinforced by his solitary 'death' in Stave 4 (6).

The Ghost of Christmas Present teaches Scrooge about what responsibility towards others means. When Scrooge, seeing how ill Tiny Tim is, asks the spirit to 'say he will be spared', he finally shows a real interest in someone else. His personal responsibility is implied when the Cratchits toast him as the 'Founder of the Feast'. At the end of the stave, his responsibility is widened to society in general when the Ghost shows him Ignorance and Want. These two children, who personify the biggest evils facing Victorian society, are 'Man's'. When the spirit paraphrases Scrooge's questions from Stave 1, asking 'Are there no prisons? ... Are there no workhouses?' he is telling Scrooge that his attitude is responsible for creating these problems (7). His warning about what might happen if Ignorance and Want are not dealt with is addressed not just to Scrooge but 'the city' and by implication to the reader. The message is clear: we must all take responsibility or face the consequences (8).

1. Opens with an effective point about how the extract relates to the idea of responsibility. AO1

2. Develops the idea of responsibility, relating it to context and using embedded quotations. AO1/AO3

3. Comments on the use of language by the writer. Reference to text related to social and historical context. AO1/AO2/AO3

4. Analysis of language, using sophisticated terminology and again relating comments to context. AO2/AO3

5. Thorough exploration of ideas about the idea of responsibility, rooted in context and using quotations effectively. AO1/AO2

6. A range of references to another part of the text, including some quotations. Thoughtful consideration of what is meant by 'responsibility', keeping focus on the question. AO1/AO2

7. Convincing response to the question, using appropriate terminology and using a quotation effectively. Analysis of structure. AO1/AO2

8. Effective ending to a coherent, thoughtful answer. AO1/AO2

Questions

EXAM PRACTICE
Spend 50 minutes writing an answer to question 3 (page 58).
Starting with this extract, explain what is meant by the spirit of Christmas and how Dickens writes about it. Write about:
• how he writes about the spirit of Christmas in the extract
• how he writes about the spirit of Christmas in the novel as a whole.
[30 marks]

Glossary

Abstract noun – a noun that is an idea or quality rather than a concrete object (such as: charity, compassion).

Active verb – a verb in the active voice, when the subject is the thing or person acting, e.g. 'the dog bit the boy'.

Adjective – a word that describes a noun.

Anaphora – to repeat a word or phrase at the beginning of successive clauses to create effect.

Adverb – a word that describes a verb.

Alliteration – a series of words beginning with the same sound.

Atmosphere – a tone, mood or general feeling.

Attitude – feeling about, or opinion of, something or someone.

Avarice – excessive desire for wealth, see page 42 for a full description.

Charwoman – a woman who earns her living from cleaning for others.

Chronological – ordered according to time.

Clause – a group of words that includes a main verb and could stand as a sentence.

Cliffhanger – ending an act or chapter with a shock or problem.

Compassion – sympathetic concern.

Connotation – to imply a meaning or suggest something by association.

Debtors' Prison – a prison people were sent to when they failed to pay their debts.

Deed – a legal document.

Denomination – a group within Christianity with its own organisation and rules.

Dowry – money which the family of an upper or a middle-class woman would pay to the man she married.

Emotive – creating or describing strong emotions.

Established Church – the official church of a country (in England, the Church of England).

The Exchange (or 'Change) – a place in the city of London where businessmen met to do deals.

Exposition – the opening part of a novel or play where setting and characters are introduced.

Fiancée – a woman engaged to be married (a man engaged to be married is a fiancé).

Flashback – a device taking a novel or play back in time.

Idealised – a version of something that is thought to be perfect.

Idol – a false god.

Image/Imagery – words used to create a picture in the imagination.

Incense – a spice which produces a sweet-smelling smoke when burned, used in religious ceremonies.

Industrialisation – the process by which (during the Industrial Revolution) the use of machinery increased, leading to big factories and causing people to leave the countryside for towns and cities in search of employment.

Imply – to suggest something that is not expressly stated.

Infer – to deduce something that is not openly stated.

Innocent – without sin.

Intrusive narrator – a narrator who comments on the action, as Dickens does in *A Christmas Carol*.

Lame – unable to walk.

Laundress – a woman who earns her living by washing clothes, etc. for others.

Ledger – a book for recording financial transactions.

Litotes – a form of ironic understatement in which a statement is made by saying what it is not, e.g. saying 'it's not my favourite' to mean 'I really hate it'.

Metaphor – an image created by writing about something as if it were something else.

Milliner – hat maker.

Minor sentence – a 'sentence' that does not contain a verb but starts with a capital letter and ends with a full stop.

Parallel phrasing – using a series of phrases with the same syntax (construction or word order) to emphasise an idea.

Pathetic fallacy – either a form of personification, giving nature human qualities, or the use of a description of surroundings to reflect the mood of a character.

Pathos – writing that causes feelings of pity or sorrow.

Penitence – feeling sorry for sins.

Personification (verb personify) – writing about an idea or object as if it were human.

Phantom – a ghost.

Philanthropist – someone (usually wealthy) who gives time and money to help others.

Plenty – abundance, especially of food.

Poor Law – a law that made parishes responsible for helping those in need. The 1834 New Poor Law severely restricted the help they could give.

Prose – any writing that is not verse.

Protagonist – the main character.

Respectable – seen as good and proper by society.

Significance – meaning, importance.

Simile – an image created by comparing one thing to another, using 'as' or 'like'.

Simple sentence – a sentence containing only one clause, including a subject and a verb.

Sin – an immoral act.

Social reform – changing society, usually with the intention of improving it.

Stanza – a division of a poem or song (also known as a verse).

Symbol – an object used to represent an idea.

Symbolise – when an object or colour represents a specific idea or meaning.

Tense – the changing of words or word endings to show when things are taking place (past, present, future).

Tradition (adj. traditional) – a long-established practice.

Transferred epithet – an adjective that should apply to a person transferred to thing, e.g. Scrooge's melancholy dinner.

Treadmill – a means of powering machinery by walking, used as punishment in prisons.

The Twelve Days of Christmas – the extended period of Christmas celebrations running from Christmas Day (25th December) to Epiphany (6th January).

Undertaker – someone who earns a living from organising funerals (now usually called a 'funeral director').

Verb – a doing, feeling, thinking or being word.

Want – need or poverty.

Workhouse – see page 22 for a detailed description.

Answers

Pages 4–5

Quick Test

1. To wish him Merry Christmas and invite him to Christmas dinner.
2. To ask for money to give to the poor.
3. Marley was Scrooge's partner. Marley has been condemned as a spirit to walk the earth forever as a ghost.
4. To get him to change his behaviour.

Exam Practice

Answers might consider how Scrooge's attitude is shown through what he says and how he acts towards others.

Analysis might include the effect of using items associated with Christmas, such as holly and pudding, in amusingly inappropriate ways, his repeated use of the word 'humbug', his disagreement with Fred, his resentment of Bob having time off and the symbolism of turning away the carol singer.

Pages 6–7

Quick Test

1. There is bright light shining from it.
2. Himself.
3. Fan is his mother.
4. His clerk (Bob Cratchit).
5. She realises that he is more in love with money than with her.

Exam Practice

Answers might focus on the contrast between Scrooge as described in Stave 1 and the descriptions of him as a boy and a young man in Stave 2, as well as the account of his changing nature in the meeting with Belle.

Analysis might include Belle's imagery when discussing his love of money, the significance of 'he sobbed' and the use of two simple sentences to convey emotion (Scrooge said he knew it. And he sobbed.), his reactions to seeing Fezziwig's party and his recognition of how he has changed by his references to his nephew Bob Cratchit, as well as to the carol singer.

Pages 8–9

Quick Test

1. He is willing to go.
2. Bob Cratchit's son.
3. Whether he will live.
4. He enjoys it.
5. Ignorance and Want.

Exam Practice

Answers might explore how the Ghost of Christmas Present represents the spirit of Christmas and the variety of scenes he shows to Scrooge.

Analysis might include Tiny Tim's reference to God being a reminder of the religious significance of Christmas, Bob's unconscious irony in calling Scrooge 'the Founder of the Feast', the Cratchits' enjoyment of what they have, the significance of the Ghost's torch, imagery of light and dark and the sense of everyone treating each other well.

Pages 10–11

Quick Test

1. The Ghost of Christmas Yet to Come.
2. Undertaker, charwoman and laundress.
3. He is shocked by their behaviour.
4. He has died.
5. Himself.

Exam Practice

Answers will centre on the contrast between the circumstances of their deaths and reactions to them.

Analysis might focus on the positive connotations of the word 'green' and the contrast with Scrooge's grave, the alliteration of 'disgust' and 'detestation' and how Scrooge's reaction reflects people's feelings about him, the use of light and dark images, the emphasis placed on Tim's innocence and goodness and the contrast between the rooms in which their bodies lie.

Pages 12–13

Quick Test

1. Christmas day.
2. A prize turkey.
3. With his nephew, Fred.
4. He will increase his pay and help his family.

Exam Practice

Answers might focus on the combination of religious observance, enjoyment and helping others. They might include the contrast of Scrooge in Stave 4 with Scrooge in Stave 1, the use of exclamations to express happiness and excitement, the detailed descriptions of food and Christmas celebrations and the way Scrooge 'makes amends' for things he did in Stave 1.

Pages 14–15

Quick Test

1. They are the divisions in a song such as a carol.
2. Chronological order.
3. He introduces Ignorance and Want.
4. He does not give the identity of the dead man and the figure of the Ghost of Christmas Yet to Come is mysterious.

Exam Practice

Answers might include the impact of the opening sentences, Dickens's role as an intrusive narrator, the exposition centring on Scrooge's character, the use of cliffhangers, the different roles of the Ghosts representing different stages in Scrooge's redemption, references made to the beginning at the end and the way 'loose ends' are tied up.

Pages 16–17

Quick Test

1. His father being in prison for debt, Dickens working in a factory.
2. He had read a government report about child labour.
3. Martha Cratchit.

Exam Practice

Analysis might include Martha's description of the long hours she works, Tiny Tim's innocence and the idea of him being sent by God, the loving relationships between parents and children, the rough and tumble of children's play, the importance of children and families at Christmas, and the reasons for and impact of the portrayal of Ignorance and Want as children.

Pages 18–19

Quick Test

1. The City of London.
2. The bright and colourful shop windows.
3. The moors where the miners live; the rocky shore and lighthouse; a ship at sea.

Exam Practice

Answers might include the use of pathetic fallacy in descriptions of Scrooge's old school and his home, association of deprivation, dirt and crime ('reeked of crime'), contrast of the 'old town' with colourful window displays and cheerful people, long sentences made up of parallel phrases building a detailed picture, contrast of wild, bleak nature and warm cosy homes.

Pages 20–21

Quick Test

1. The middle class.
2. Millinery, charwoman and laundress.
3. Vote in elections; own property when married.
4. Any two of: Fan/Belle/Mrs Cratchit/Mrs Fezziwig/Caroline.

Exam Practice

Answers might include how Mrs Cratchit is defined by her role (we do not know her first name) and is devoted to her family, how both she and Belle manage large families while their husbands work, Mrs Cratchit's cooking of the Christmas dinner, Belle's choice of love over money, the dancing of the Fezziwigs showing their love and enjoyment, Fred's wife's role as a 'young housekeeper' and the way all the wives are rewarded by the love of their husbands and children.

Pages 22–23

Quick Test

1. Industrialisation and increasing population.
2. Breaking stones and crushing bones.
3. Let people die through famine and disease.
4. Revolution.

Exam Practice

Answers might include the way the beggars' dogs avoid him, his refusal to give to charity, his 'grasping' nature, his belief that Fred is too poor to marry, his belief that poverty is none of his business, his assertion that the provisions of the Poor Law are adequate and his lack of consideration for the poor as humans shown by his statement that they had better die.

Pages 24–25

Quick Test

1. About half.
2. Through faith (or prayer) and good works.
3. Dance and drink alcohol.
4. The Ten Commandments of the Old Testament and Christ's teaching in the New Testament.

Exam Practice

Answers might include:

Fred – acknowledges the religious significance of Christmas, invites Scrooge to his house, entertains his family and friends, loves his wife, feels sorry for Scrooge.

Mr Fezziwig – treats his employees well, is generous to his friends and neighbours, is a good family man.

Bob Cratchit – celebrates Christmas, goes to church, looks after his family, accepts Tiny Tim's illness and 'death', shows a Christian attitude to Scrooge.

Pages 26–27

Quick Test

1. Red; blue; and white.
2. Scrooge's fiancée.
3. No. He is shown enjoying Christmas at Mr Fezziwig's party.
4. Protagonist.

Exam Practice

Answers might explore Scrooge's meanness, his solitariness and his hatred of Christmas.

Analysis could include the way the description of his physical appearance is linked to his character, the use of strings of adjectives, the use of metaphors and similes, his treatment of Bob Cratchit, his reaction to Fred's invitation, his use of the phrase 'Bah! Humbug!', his reaction to the charity collectors and the carol singer, the description of his home and his behaviour after leaving the counting house.

Pages 28–29

Quick Test

1. Seeing himself as a lonely boy.
2. He says that he cannot bear to see any more.
3. By changing his behaviour and learning the lessons the Ghosts have taught him.
4. Generous; happy; popular.

Exam Practice

Answers should focus on the contrast between Scrooge in Stave 1 and Scrooge in Stave 5.

Analysis might focus on the change in the way he moves and speaks, the way he talks to himself and about himself, using words such as 'giddy' and 'merry', the frequent use of exclamations, his actions towards the Cratchits, his visit to Fred, his meeting with the charitable gentlemen and what Dickens tells us about how his life changes.

Answers

Pages 30–31
Quick Test
1. Any three from: cash boxes; keys; ledgers; deeds; purses; padlocks.
2. Travel the earth tortured by remorse.
3. A cap and a sprig of holly.
4. He struggles with it and tries to extinguish its flame.

Exam Practice
Answers could explore how the Ghost helps Scrooge to understand how he has changed and to experience feelings that he had in the past and to connect what he sees with his present life.

Analysis might include the following: the meaning of the tear that Scrooge sheds; pathetic fallacy in the description of the school; the contrast between Fezziwig and older Scrooge; the description of Fezziwig's party, using repetition, adjectives and adverb; Belle's language when she talks to Scrooge about his love of money; the use of the first person intrusive narrator in the description of Belle's family; the symbolism of the Ghost's light.

Pages 32–33
Quick Test
1. It sprinkles incense on dinners and on people.
2. For the twelve days of Christmas.
3. A green robe trimmed with white fur and a holly wreath on its head.
4. One arm/hand.

Exam Practice
Analysis might include the following: the symbolism associated with their appearance; the idea of 'plenty' connected to Christmas Present; the linking of Christmas traditions and religion; the significance of Christmas Present's torch; the idea of the spirit of Christmas; the Ghost's repetition of things Scrooge has said; how seeing others celebrating affects Scrooge; the shocking revelation of Ignorance and Want and its meaning; the association of Christmas Yet to Come with death; the effect of the Ghost not speaking; the mystery around the dead man; the shock and pathos of Tim's death.

Pages 34–35
Quick Test
1. Martha, Peter, Tiny Tim and Belinda.
2. Mrs Cratchit is angry with him but Bob is not.
3. He thinks that seeing him would remind them of the teachings of Christ.
4. 'Patient' and 'mild'.

Exam Practice
Answers might focus on their closeness and mutual support, their ability to enjoy Christmas and how seeing them at Christmas changes Scrooge. Analysis might include the use of adjectives such as 'mild' to describe Bob and Tiny Tim, the Cratchits as an example of poor people, the description of activity and cooperation, the details of their poverty (turned over dress, glasses) and their enjoyment of a modest dinner (goose, small pudding).

Pages 36–37
Quick Test
1. Married.
2. Any two from: He is generous/he is cheerful/he enjoys Christmas.
3. It makes them think of others.
4. Things are much better at home.

Exam Practice
Answers might focus on how Fred is contrasted with Scrooge, how he differs in his attitude to Christmas, is outgoing and generous, and has a happy home life. Analysis could include the way he speaks, his enthusiasm shown by exclamations, his laughter, his sympathetic and forgiving attitude to Scrooge. Answers could also mention his mother and how Fred feels a sense of responsibility to Scrooge but it is not returned.

Pages 38–39
Quick Test
1. He is his employer/Scrooge is apprenticed to him.
2. He throws a party at Christmas.
3. She has not got any money and he now loves money more than he loves her.
4. She has a family, while he is alone. She is happy but he is not.

Exam Practice
Analysis might focus on Belle's language to Scrooge, including her use of personification ('Gain') and religious imagery ('idol') to her situation in life. Her awareness of how Scrooge has changed, her understanding of the importance of love, her sense of honour, how her later life shows what Scrooge has missed and the importance of family life.

Pages 40–41
Quick Test
1. The Ghost of Christmas Present.
2. By casting incense from its torch.
3. By collecting money to help the poor.
4. By throwing a party for his employees, family and friends.

Exam Practice
Answers could focus on Fred, Mr Fezziwig, the Cratchits or the portly gentlemen. They might mention the enjoyment of the season, the focus on family and friends, religious observance and generosity towards others. They could analyse what characters say about Christmas, for example, Fred's speech to Scrooge or Bob's account of Tiny Tim in church or the portly gentlemen's explanation of why they are collecting.

Page 42–43
Quick Test
1. Greed/ pursuit of money or wealth.
2. No, but excessive desire for it and not putting it to good use are.
3. Someone who hoards wealth and lives miserably.
4. Gain or the acquisition of wealth.

Exam Practice
Analysis might include the use of the phrase 'tight-fisted' to sum up Scrooge's attitude to money, Belle's use of religious imagery ('idol'), Scrooge's meanness in not having enough coal for the fire and not giving to charity and Scrooge as a miser who does not enjoy his wealth. Contrast this with Fred and the Cratchits, who make the most of what they have, as well as with Fezziwig's generosity.

Pages 44–45
Quick Test
1. From under the robes of the Ghost of Christmas Present.
2. They look old; they appear possessed by devils rather than angels.
3. Man (humanity).
4. Doom.

Exam Practice
Analysis might focus on the comparison of the personification of ideas as children to animals ('wolfish', 'claw'), use of emotive language such as 'monsters', contrast with Victorian ideals of childhood, the way their appearances change the mood of the novel, the Ghost's warning and his use of imperatives.

Pages 46–47
Quick Test
1. The Cratchits; Belle's family.
2. Christmas is traditionally seen as a time for families and children.
3. Four.
4. He leaves him alone at school at Christmas.

Exam Practice
Answers could focus on the contrast with Scrooge's isolation, the details of the Cratchits' Christmas dinner and each family member's contribution, the rough and tumble of Belle's family, the use of exclamations and the intrusive narrator, the sadness of Scrooge's childhood contrasted with the other children described and the love within families in happy and sad times.

Pages 48–49
Quick Test
1. Uncaring, glad.
2. Nobody.
3. 'Reconciled' or content.
4. Marley's.

Exam Practice
Answers should focus on the contrast between the circumstances of, and reactions to, the 'deaths' of Scrooge and Tiny Tim. They might analyse the eeriness of the descriptions of Scrooge's deathbed and grave, emotive language, use of adjectives, direct address to personified Death, the gentle language used at Tim's deathbed, contrasting attitudes shown in conversations about Scrooge and Tim, the idea that goodness lives on and the way the Cratchits accept Tim's death.

Pages 50–51
Quick Test
1. He is Bob's employer and so could pay him more, which might help to pay for better medical care.
2. Scrooge.
3. The portly gentlemen.
4. All human beings.

Exam Practice
Answers might focus on Scrooge's personal responsibility and/or people's responsibility to each other in general. They might mention the contrast of Scrooge with those who have a sense of responsibility, e.g. Mr Fezziwig, Scrooge's refusal to take responsibility in Stave 1 and the repetition of his words about workhouses and prisons, his responsibility for the Cratchits' problems, his responsibility for his own state and the Ghost of Christmas Present's address to 'Man'.

Pages 52–53
Quick Test
1. Avarice (or Greed).
2. As an innocent child, Tim is linked to Jesus Christ, born on Christmas day.
3. The events described in Stave 4 do not happen.

Exam Practice
Answers might refer to the description of Scrooge as a 'covetous old sinner' and the sin of avarice, to Marley's ghost and his punishment, the association of Tiny Tim with the child Jesus, the implication of Scrooge feeling guilt in his references to Fred and Bob in Stave 2 and his changed behaviour in Stave 5.

Pages 56-61
Exam Practice
Use the mark scheme on page 80 to self-assess your strengths and weaknesses. The estimated grade boundaries are included so you can assess your progress towards your target grade.

Pages 62–63
Quick Test
1. Understanding of the whole text, specific analysis and terminology, awareness of the relevance of context, a well-structured essay and accurate writing.
2. Planning focuses your thoughts and allows you to produce a well-structured essay.
3. Quotations give you more opportunities to do specific AO2 analysis.

Exam Practice
Ideas might include the following: Fred is cheerful and outgoing in contrast to Scrooge; he reaches out to Scrooge; he enjoys Christmas and celebrates it with his family; he cares about love more than money; he understands the spirit of Christmas and links celebration with its religious meaning; he is hospitable and kind, his home being warm and welcoming, unlike Scrooge's; his link to Fan; the way the Cratchits talk about him in Stave 4.

Answers

Pages 66–67 and 72–73

Exam Practice

Use the mark scheme below to self-assess your strengths and weaknesses. Work up from the bottom, putting a tick by things you have fully accomplished, a ½ by skills that are in place but need securing and underlining areas that need particular development. The estimated grade boundaries are included so you can assess your progress towards your target grade.

Pages 68–69

Quick Test

1. Understanding of the whole text, specific analysis and terminology, awareness of the relevance of context, a well-structured essay and accurate writing.
2. Planning focuses your thoughts and allows you to produce a well-structured essay.
3. Quotations give you more opportunities to do specific AO2 analysis.

Exam Practice

Ideas might include the following: contrast of weather and landscape with homely scene; focus on family; people enjoying themselves despite poverty; how Christmas transforms the old man; tradition in the Christmas songs; symbolism of light; contrast between situation of miners and lighthouse men but all keep Christmas; link celebration to religious significance; the Ghost of Christmas Present as a symbolic figure; the Ghost's torch used to spread the spirit of Christmas; Christmas honoured by helping others, showing love to family and strangers.

Grade	AO1 (12 marks)	AO2 (12 marks)	AO3 (6 marks)
6–7+	A convincing, well-structured essay that answers the question fully. Quotations and references are well chosen and integrated into sentences. The response covers the whole novel.	Analysis of the full range of Dickens's methods. Thorough exploration of the effects of these methods. Accurate range of subject terminology.	Exploration is linked to specific aspects of the novel's contexts to show a detailed understanding.
4–5	A clear essay that always focuses on the exam question. Quotations and references support ideas effectively. The response refers to different points in the novel.	Explanation of Dickens's different methods. Clear understanding of the effects of these methods. Accurate use of subject terminology.	References to relevant aspects of context show a clear understanding.
2–3	The essay has some good ideas that are mostly relevant. Some quotations and references are used to support the ideas.	Identification of some different methods used by Dickens to convey meaning. Some subject terminology.	Some awareness of how ideas in the novel link to its context.